Mor...
Fashions

Also available in Beaver

Freaky Fashions by Caroline Archer
Jazzy Jewellery by Lynda Perkin
and Heather Dewhurst

More Freaky Fashions

Caroline Archer

Illustrated by Jane Brook

BEAVER BOOKS

A Beaver Book
Published by Arrow Books Limited
62–5 Chandos Place, London WC2N 4NW

An imprint of Century Hutchinson Ltd

London Melbourne Sydney Auckland
Johannesburg and agencies throughout the world

First published 1989

Text © Complete Editions Ltd 1989
Illustrations © Century Hutchinson Ltd 1989

Set in Palatino
by JH Graphics Ltd, Reading

Printed and bound in Great Britain by
Courier International Ltd, Tiptree, Essex

ISBN 0 09 964900 4

Contents

1. Looking Good, Feeling Good

Most people care about the appearance they present to the world, and if you are reading this book you must be one of them. You may want simply to impress people with your good looks and your flair for clever dressing, or you may want to convey an image of being a certain type of person — perhaps someone who is mysterious and exciting, or someone who is fun to be with, or simply, when it comes to leaving school and finding a job, someone who is sensible and efficient.

But there's more to it than that. If you know you look right (and this may depend on the occasion — what looks right for watching a weekend football match would not look right for attending your sister's wedding!) you tend to feel right, and if you feel right you will have more self-confidence, which will, in turn, give people confidence in you. So, apart from the fun angle, it is worth spending a bit of time (and, unfortunately, money!) on getting things right.

Where should you start? Well, first of all set aside a day at the weekend or in the holidays to get everything out of your wardrobe and have a good look at it. Anything you've bought in the past and really hate and consequently never wear you should throw out, though do check first that your parents don't mind! You might also consider giving things away to friends, or swapping clothes that don't suit you for something that doesn't suit them. However, anything that just seems a bit dull or boring keep on one side, for when you have read this book you should have some ideas for how to make these clothes more exciting.

The major part of fashion sense lies in having a feeling for what goes with what. It isn't necessary to have lots of clothes, but if you have the right things to go with them, a limited number of fairly ordinary garments can be turned into lots of different and exciting outfits.

So lay out all your possible clothes and take a good look at them. If it's the middle of summer you may not want to think about your heaviest jumpers and coats, but if it is winter don't discard your summer things because you can often wear them under, or over, other clothes. Your summer shorts, for instance, can be worn over a pair of thick tights or leggings in winter; and T-shirts are always useful under shirts and jumpers for warmth as well as for effect. Even a summer dress can be worn over a T-shirt and leggings to brighten up a winter day.

With all your clothes laid out, collect together all the bits and pieces that go with them − hats, gloves, scarves, hair bands, jewellery, tights, socks and leggings − and see what goes with what, and what contrasts with what. Colour is very important here. If you want to look smart, you can choose colours that tone with or complement each other, such as pink and grey, or colours that contrast directly with each other, such as scarlet and navy. If, on the other hand, you feel like looking freaky, you could wear pink with orange or scarlet. (See chapter 3 for more about colour.)

Putting all your clothes and accessories together like this should give you fresh ideas about what you can do with them. Often people wear the same jumper with the same pair of trousers or skirt and don't realize how well it would go with something else. This kind of stock-taking enables you to assemble all kinds of possible outfits and spot what, if anything, is missing from them. That's the time to take out your notebook and pencil and make a shopping list.

Don't forget to include your school clothes in your stock-taking. You may be surprised at how easily you can disguise their origins when you wear them with other clothes and accessories.

Working out what goes with what is a bit of a mathematical problem, but here is an example. Leaving out overcoats and raincoats, which may be worn for practical reasons rather than style (though there is no reason why they should not be stylish too), let us suppose your wardrobe consists of:

Three T-shirts: one white, one red, one yellow
Six blouses/shirts: three white (school), one blue and white striped, one pink flowered
Four sweaters: one navy V-necked, one red, one blue, one polo-necked black
Four pairs of trousers: one blue jeans, one mid-calf length yellow, one black, one jade green
One party dress
One summer dress in bright colours

Four skirts: one navy, one black, one red and
   yellow (summer), one denim
One black jacket
One light-coloured jacket
Various scarves, tights, leggings, socks, belts,
   etc.

Here are some ways in which the clothes could be
combined to provide an exciting, fun wardrobe.

- Yellow T-shirt with yellow mid-calf pants, and
  a bright red and orange scarf tied round the
  middle, or a broad fuchsia or jade green belt, or
  a broad black belt with black necklace and
  earrings.
- Pink-flowered blouse and the red and yellow
  summer skirt with a broad orange belt round
  the middle. Or, for winter, black polo-necked
  sweater under the blouse, black tights or
  leggings under the skirt, and broad black belt
  round the middle. Pink or red earrings.
- Red sweater over blue and white striped shirt,
  blue jeans, red striped socks, broad leather (or
  leather-look) belt, large blue earrings.
- Navy V-necked sweater over yellow T-shirt,
  green trousers, broad yellow belt or scarf,
  green earrings, green or navy socks.
- Polo-necked black sweater with black skirt or
  trousers, black sheer tights with skirt, diamanté
  earrings and necklace and party make-up for a
  special occasion.
- Pink-flowered shirt over white T-shirt with
  navy or denim skirt, blue jeans or black
  trousers, with broad pink belt and pink
  socks/tights.

- On a cool day you could wear the summer dress over a T-shirt and a blouse, too, if necessary, and thick tights which pick out one of the colours in its pattern or contrast brightly. For example, a blue and white dress could be worn over navy tights or bright red ones, or even dark green or yellow.
- Pink-flowered shirt over blue sweater with blue jeans, denim skirt, navy skirt or green trousers, with broad fuchsia belt and pink tights or socks.
- Light-coloured jacket over yellow T-shirt and jade trousers, with plain leather or leather-look belt and green earrings.
- Light-coloured jacket over red sweater and denim skirt, with red tights, red belt and red earrings.

There are lots of alternatives, the permutations being almost endless. You may not like the examples I have suggested, or may feel that you could rearrange the clothes much better. If so, go ahead, for that is what this book is all about! But I hope the exercise will show you that there are lots of things you can do with your existing clothes, without having to spend a great deal of money. If you buy or make one or two belts, some bright tights and scarves, some cheap but effective jewellery, and so on, you can create a number of exciting new looks simply and cheaply.

In the first *Freaky Fashions* book I explained how you could decorate your clothes by sewing and craft techniques, such as patching, quilting, embroidery, tie and dye and colour printing. This information cannot be repeated in this book, but

11

the fact that these techniques are available and are cheap and easy to do, should be borne in mind. For example, a plain T-shirt or sweater can be brightened up by embroidering a pattern on it (easier than knitting a patterned sweater), a shirt can have a pocket of a contrasting colour sewn on it, a skirt may have a band of contrasting material sewn round the hem, or lace sewn on to make a false petticoat. Even if you are not very good with a needle, these things are not difficult to do, and just require a little time and patience.

2. Know Yourself

Adult books and articles about fashion always say that you should assess yourself and your lifestyle before trying to decide what kind of clothes are right for you. And, to a lesser extent, this also applies to you, for though you may sometimes feel that your life consists of nothing but school, in your spare time you have as individual a lifestyle as any adult. And in deciding what kind of clothes are right for you, this lifestyle has to be taken into account. Do you go to lots of parties and discos? Do you take part in a lot of sports? Is your ideal spare time activity just pottering around at home with your friends? Do you have a weekend job, and does it demand that you dress in a certain way? All these things have to be considered, especially if you have to work out your own budget for buying clothes. If you like parties but have to spend money on clothes for playing tennis in, or riding at the weekends, you might do better to spend your money on a couple of exciting outfits for parties and discos rather than trying to stretch it to buy the sports gear, the party clothes *and* snazzy daytime clothes. On the other hand, if you don't like parties and don't need clothes for special activities, then you may prefer to concentrate on casual, go-everywhere clothes that make you feel good whatever you are doing.

For some weekend jobs you may need to wear clothes that are neat and tidy, and seem almost as boring as school uniforms. But I think you'll find that as long as you are reasonably neat and tidy your employer will actually prefer you to wear interesting clothes. He or she may draw the line at outrageous make-up and hairstyles, but will probably prefer to see someone in brightly coloured neat clothes that have obviously been selected with some care, than someone dressed in a shapeless grey pullover and a scruffy pair of jeans.

You must also decide what kind of clothes you feel happy in. Some girls like wearing skirts; others always wear trousers. Some like dresses; some blouses and skirts. Some hate wearing tights and go around bare-legged in cold weather; others shudder at the thought and wear thick tights or trousers with boots at the first sign of autumn. While you should never give in to natural laziness and always slop around in an old jumper and a pair of jeans, if you are happiest in trousers it may be as well to concentrate on them and make them look attractive, rather than just wearing them with any old jumper, or, even worse, forcing yourself into wearing a dress you don't like and are not happy in but wear because everything else looks too awful.

A good way of finding out what you like to wear and feel you look good in is to imagine that someone you really admire is taking you out somewhere. How would you see yourself dressing, assuming you could have anything you wanted? Would you dress in the most outrageous colours and styles you can imagine, or would you wear something you thought suggested good taste and elegance? It all depends what sort of person you are, but the answer to this question will help you to know yourself and so decide what types of clothes you should concentrate on.

You may think that if you don't wear the latest fashions your friends will notice and think you are behind the times, but if instead you wear something that looks good and you feel good in it, they will actually think more of you than if you are going around looking fashionable but feeling unhappy about it. It takes a bit of courage to stand out for what you believe in when you are young, but it is those who do so who become the leaders of fashion instead of its followers.

Your physical appearance

Part of this self-assessment of what suits you lies in defining your body type. Nowadays it is fashionable to be thin, but thirty or forty years ago the fashion idols of today would have been considered emaciated, whereas the sex symbols of those days were, by today's standards, chubby. Look at films of the 1950s with stars such as Marilyn Monroe and Jane Russell. Not only did they have big bosoms, but they were well-covered all over, and considered the ultimate in desirability. So body shape is a matter of fashion, too, and if yours isn't ideal, then don't worry about it. The secret lies in trying to hide your bad points and emphasize your good ones. As long as you aren't unhealthily over- or underweight, it is better to accept yourself as you are, rather than adopt drastic diets or other extreme solutions.

You can assess your shape and type by looking in a mirror, but often you will get a much more objective viewpoint if you study photographs of yourself. Then you will not only be able to judge your height and weight, but also the way you sit or stand, whether you are upright or round-shouldered, whether you hollow your back and stick out your tummy, etc. Take a good hard look and try to see what are your good points and what your bad. *Are* your shoulders round? Is your bosom small — or big? Is your waist large in comparison with your hips, or vice versa? Do you have a short body and long legs, or the other way around? And while you are being so critical with yourself, don't forget your good points, too. You may be a little wide in the hips, but still have lovely long, shapely legs. Your waist may be too big for the ideal, but perhaps your bosom is very shapely. You may have large feet, but beautifully coloured hair or eyes. The idea is to try to wear clothes that bring out these good points, and hide the bad ones.

Creating optical illusions

Many people will be familiar with simple optical illusions like those in the diagrams opposite. In the top drawing the second line appears longer than the first, because of the direction of the arrows at its ends, though both lines are the same length. The square outside the circle looks smaller than that inside it, though they are the same size; the rectangle divided vertically looks taller and narrower than that divided horizontally. Similarly the rectangle with two vertical lines close together looks narrower than that with the lines further apart.

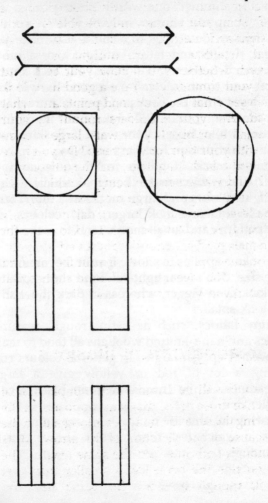

These illusions can be used to advantage if you want to appear to be taller, shorter, slimmer or fatter than you really are. A pattern of vertical stripes on a dress or shirt will make you appear taller and slimmer; one with horizontal lines will make you appear shorter and fatter. If the vertical lines form wide stripes this could also make you appear shorter and fatter. A V-neck or a scoop neck on a dress or top will make your neck appear longer and your face more slender, as will hair taken away from the neck and face. A short jacket, or a contrasting belt, will make a tall figure look shorter, while loose clothes and full skirts will make a thin person look less scrawny.

Printed fabrics tend to make someone look larger; plain fabrics make them look smaller. Light or bright colours and large motifs in a fabric tend to make someone look larger; dark colours, all-over patterns and small motifs tend to make them look smaller.

The same applies to shoes. If your feet are on the large size, don't wear light-coloured shoes, or they will look even bigger, whereas in dark shoes they will look smaller.

Shiny fabrics, such as satin, rough, textured fabrics and hand-knitted woollens all tend to make the wearer appear larger. In general, colours containing a lot of red or yellow give a larger appearance, while those based on blues give a smaller one.

Bearing all this in mind, here are some basic ways in which less than perfect figures can be camouflaged.

Tall and thin

Clothes that curve in some way are ideal, as are loose clothes 'cut' across the middle or the hips by a contrasting belt or scarf. Full skirts, wide collars, or a shawl or scarf round the shoulders, and bright, warm colours with contrasts at the waist and hips all help.

Tall and well-built

Those who are large and strongly built should avoid hard-looking tailored clothes, and go for gentle flaring or draped shapes, which give softness, and diagonal lines. Subdued colours, that are neither too dark nor too bright, help too. Large patterns on fabrics, and shiny materials, should be avoided.

Short and slim

Designs with vertical lines, or diagonally vertical lines, help. Tops should be kept short and skirts longish, e.g. tuck in sweaters rather than wearing them over the skirt of trousers. It is best to wear one colour with, say, a matching belt, rather than going in for contrasts. Designs and fabrics should be chosen so they are light in feel and colour, and not overpowering in texture or design.

Short and chubby

Vertical or diagonally vertical lines help. Short jackets and belts that 'cut you in half' should be avoided, as should bright colours, heavy, chunky fabrics and designs, and shiny materials.

Large hips

Avoid tight skirts and trousers, and instead wear looser ones. Avoid also lines which cut across the hips, such as a low-slung belt. To draw the eye away from the hips, add points of interest elsewhere, such as a scarf at the neck, or a brooch pinned at the neck or shoulder.

Small bosom

Tops with gathers below the bosom, bloused and draped bodices, and overblouses all help. You could also cheat and pad out your bra.

Short-waisted

This means that the body between the waist and shoulders is comparatively short. Long jackets, overshirts, and one-colour clothes with smooth lines help to hide it; contrasting belts and very full or very narrow skirts emphasize it.

Long-waisted

This, of course, is the opposite problem, and here wide, contrasting belts and sashes work wonders. Peplum jackets (those that fit tightly into the waist and have a little frilled hem), help too.

Narrow shoulders

Shoulder pads were a boon to narrow-shouldered people, though they are not as popular as they once were. You could, however, make or buy small pads and attach them to different garments, or to your bra straps.

Short neck

Collars that stand away from the neck and lowered necklines help here. High collars make matters worse.

Long neck

Here polo-necked sweaters are very useful, as are large collars and choker necklaces.

Sticking-out tummy

If you think your tummy sticks out too much you should check your posture. Look at yourself in the mirror. Does your tummy stick out, your bottom stick out, and have you a deep hollow in your back above it? If so, this is not only bad for your shape,

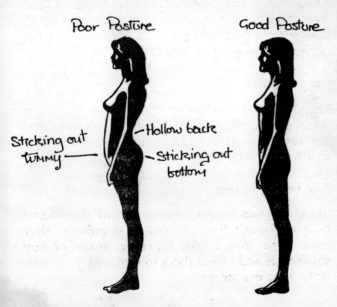

Poor Posture   Good Posture

Sticking out tummy —

— Hollow back

— Sticking out bottom

it can put a strain on your back too. Try tucking in your tummy and bottom, and trying to flatten out the hollow above your bottom, which is called the lumbar curve. You will then have a much better, more upright posture and lessen the chances of getting backache. Try to remember to keep doing this when you find yourself standing badly, especially if you have to keep standing for some time. Vertical lines, and hip-length overshirts, jumpers and jackets help, too.

Sticking-out bottom

The same advice for posture correction applies here. Hip-length tops with flared skirts help to disguise it. Trousers should only be worn with long, loose overshirts or sweaters, or you will look awful!

3. Colour Counsel

Colour is terribly important in our lives, and finding out which colours you like and which suit you best is an important part of fashion. Light can be broken up into seven colours: red, orange, yellow, green, blue, indigo and violet, but, in fact, there are only three primary colours — red, yellow and blue — from which all other colours can be made. For example, orange is made from mixing red and yellow, green from blue and yellow.

Blues, blue-greens, greens and blue-purples are said to be 'cool' colours; reds, oranges, yellows and red-purples are 'warm' colours. The warm colours are said to advance, i.e. they seem to be nearer to you than they are; the cool colours to recede. Black, white, grey, dark navy and brown are considered neutral colours, and it is on these that women are always told to base their wardrobes. This may sound dull, but unless you adore a particular bright colour and always want to wear it, it makes sense to buy expensive items of clothing, like a winter coat, in a neutral colour. That way you are less likely to tire of it the following year, and it can always be dressed up with brightly coloured scarves, tights, and so on.

As you will know if you have ever done any painting, all kinds of shades can be created by mixing colours. Colours may be bright, or they may be subdued, an effect created by the addition of grey. Again, this may sound dull, but it can create lovely soft colours which suit a lot of people better than do the brighter ones.

Colour can have a profound effect on people's moods and feelings. In general, it is said that casual wear and warm colours draw people towards you and encourage them to confide in you. Light colours are said to attract the eye, and can therefore be used to draw attention to a good point and away from a bad one. For example, if you have a nicely shaped bosom but are a bit heavy round the hips, a light-coloured top and a dark skirt would draw the attention to the right place. Dark colours, such as black, navy and dark grey, signify authority – a fact you may remember when job-hunting! Red gives the impression of action and drama, green of calmness and peace; blue is calm and cool, as is light grey; pink is romantic and said to encourage protective feelings in men. Yellow, with its connotations of springtime, is bright and fresh, orange is cheerful, and brown steady and reliable.

In recent years people have made careful studies of colour and how it affects the way we dress. They say that we all have either a blue tone to our skin, hair and eyes, or a golden one, and within these two groups we can be subdivided into four basic types, which they name after the seasons – spring, summer, autumn and winter. The springs and autumns are the golden-toned people; the summers and winters the blue-toned, and each group is said to look best in colours based on their tones.

*

One way of finding out your colour type is to get together with your friends, each of whom should bring some clothing in 'solid', i.e. not patterned, colours — with as many different colours and shades of the colours as possible. Sort the clothing into colours and shades, and then take turns to drape them across the front and neck of your bodies, next to the face. Assess the effect each colour has. Does it drain the colour from your face, or enhance it? Does it make you look tired, or glowing? Does it bring out the colour of your eyes, or 'lose' them? You shouldn't be wearing make-up when you try this test, for it can confuse the issue. As each person has a go, keep the colours that suit them on one side, and then, at the end, see if they have anything in common. Are they all clear, bright colours, or muted shades? Are they predominantly blue-toned or golden-toned?

If, from this exercise, you can clearly see which shades suit you best, then try to remember the colours, or, if you have some paints or crayons, try and reproduce them as exactly as possible on a sheet of paper. Then, when you do go shopping for new clothes, take the colour swatches with you and buy things that correspond with them. But don't ever buy a colour you don't like, even if you are convinced it suits you. The chances are you will never feel happy with it, and if you don't feel happy, you won't look good.

4. A to Z of Freaky Fashion Ideas

Antique shops

An antique shop may be the last place you would think of when looking for fashion ideas, but you might be pleasantly surprised. There are shops that sell antique clothing exclusively, but there are lots of other shops — those of the old junk variety, rather than the polished Chippendale sort — which from time to time stock items of clothing. You may find delicately embroidered petticoats and nighties, wonderful fringed shawls, a beaded evening bag, or sometimes an elaborate evening dress. Old jewellery is also worth hunting out, though this can be very expensive. But sometimes you may find strings of beads, or old brooches that are beautiful and affordable.

Appliqué

This means sewing or sticking small motifs made from a similar or contrasting fabric on to a garment. For example, you could decorate a breast pocket with a cut-out and sewn-on apple, a bunch of cherries, a hippopotamus, or a daisy. If your artistic powers are not too good, then it is as well to stick to simple shapes. Draw and cut out a shape slightly larger than you wish the finished result to be, to allow you to turn in a hem all the way round to stop the picture fraying. Remember that if the garment you are sewing it on is washable, then the motif has to be made of a washable fabric, too, or the garment may be ruined. If it is normally dry cleaned, make the appliqué item from non-washable felt. (For more details about appliqué, see *Freaky Fashions*.)

Army surplus/camping shops

These can be a good source of fairly cheap things like sweatshirts, jumpers, cotton and corduroy trousers and jeans, windcheater-type jackets, woolly socks, cotton hats, and so on, all of which can be jazzed up in some of the ways mentioned in this book to create something a little more special.

Beads

Beads can be bought in lots of different colours and sizes, and one or two different shapes. They can be sewn on to a dress or sweater to create a pattern, used to create necklaces, bracelets, hair bands, and belts by weaving or sewing, or even glued on to

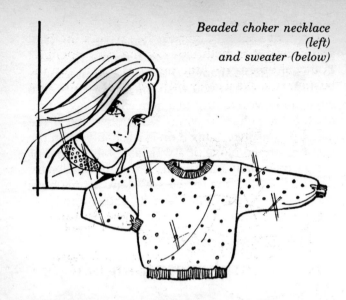

*Beaded choker necklace
(left)
and sweater (below)*

existing plain belts or stiff ribbon, such as peter-sham, to make a belt or choker necklace. Small 'pearls' can also be used in the same way.

Bustiers

These are the tight, strapless garments that look like long-line bras, and are very fashionable. They are also rather expensive for what they are. You could make your own, however, with some stretchy, shiny, clinging fabric and a strapless bra. Sew the fabric lightly over and round the top of the bra, then sew lightly round and under the cups, too. At the back, leave an opening that you can hem and sew small press-studs on, and turn up a hem at the bottom. If the bottom of the bustier doesn't fit snugly enough, thread a piece of narrow, but not too tight elastic through the hem and secure it at both sides of the back opening. You could then sew little beads or sequins on the bustier, to make a top which will look terrific with

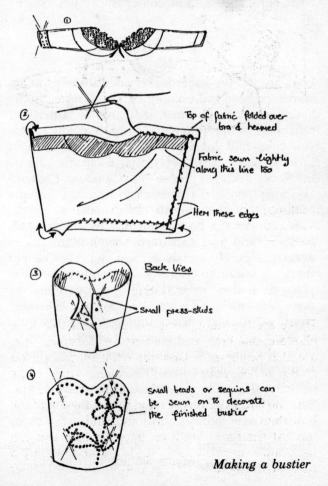

①

② Top of fabric folded over bra & hemmed

Fabric sewn lightly along this line too

Hem these edges

③ Back View

Small press-studs

④ Small beads or sequins can be sewn on to decorate the finished bustier

Making a bustier

a swirly skirt or loose trousers for evening wear. If the thought of all that exposed flesh makes you feel cold, or if your skin isn't as beautiful as you would like it to be, wear a tight black polo-neck sweater, or a body stocking, underneath it and wear tights of the same colour under your skirt.

Buttons

Look around the haberdashery departments of big stores for new and exciting button designs. Some look like sweets or fruits, ladybirds or butterflies; others are simply huge and brightly coloured. Or you may find lovely old buttons on clothes in jumble sales and secondhand shops. Some markets, such as those at Camden Lock in London, have stalls devoted to beautiful antique buttons, though these may be expensive.

A garment can be transformed by changing its buttons, and you can even sew buttons on to garments purely for decoration, whether or not there are buttonholes. They can simply be sewn in place as if they were fastening the garment, or sewn on to make a design. A narrow panel created from two parallel lines of buttons down the front of a garment creates a slimming effect.

Another idea is to make unusual earrings out of two really attractive buttons.

'Cheap and nasty' shops

There may be some shops which sell cheap clothes that you and your friends wouldn't dream of looking for ideas or clothes in. (You know the kind — they sell such things as shapeless Crimplene dresses in lurid colours!) But don't rule them out entirely. They are always worth a look, for sometimes you may find something unexpected that could look really attractive, when worn with your clothes.

Dressmaking

No, don't groan, for you can buy some very simple patterns nowadays with which to create great effects. To start with, you can try making the super-simple designs on pages 72 to 82. You don't necessarily need a sewing machine (*anyone* can hand-sew with a bit of practice) and dressmaking is a very good way of creating the kind of clothes you want in the fabrics and colours you like. You can, for example, make a gathered skirt for winter or summer with a couple of metres of 100cm or 130cm fabric by sewing the side seams, turning over the top and running a length of elastic through it to make a waistband, and then turning up the hem at the bottom to the length you require. The great thing about making your own clothes is that you can choose exactly the fabric and colours you like, and add any decorative touches you fancy.

Dyeing

Dyeing clothes used to be a complicated business, but nowadays dyes are available that can be used in the washing machine and make your fabric colour fast even to boiling. But do check first with your mother that it is OK to use the washing machine, even though the dyes are not supposed to leave any residue. She would be very cross if her best white blouse came out pink.

Dyeing can turn quite ordinary garments such as T-shirts and plain blouses into clothes that really catch the eye because of their colour. Stunning colours that you cannot easily buy – deep purples, hot pinks, greeny-blues, deep golds, and so on – can be created easily and simply and with the minimum of expenditure. Or you can simply dye things whatever your favourite colour happens to be (but bear in mind that the following year you may have changed your mind, so don't dye everything mauve!).

It always seems that if I want something in a particular colour I can never find it in the shops, especially if it is not one of the particular season's favourites. But with a range of colourful dyes to hand it is easy to buy something white and then turn it into the colour you want.

If the garment isn't white to start with, however, you have to be a bit careful. For example, you cannot dye a red shirt blue, it would simply go a purply colour, and with many attempts at dyeing one colour another colour, you end up with a muddy brown. You can only dye things a darker shade of what they already are, not a totally different colour. (For example, pink may be dyed red, but not green.)

Embroidery

If you are any good at sewing, you can embroider a design on to a plain blouse, sweater or dress, but bear in mind that it needn't necessarily mean neat little flowers worked in silk thread. You can embroider a bold message on a plain sweater — such as 'Hello!' on the front and 'Goodbye!' on the back — so it looks as if it is knitted in the design. Messages can be written out first on the fabric using tailor's chalk and then sewn on in wool, using a large needle or a bodkin, and stem or chain stitch. (For more details about embroidery, see *Freaky Fashions*.)

'Embroidery paste'

This is the most wonderful way of cheating you can imagine. If you like the thought of an embroidered pattern, but are too lazy or too clumsy to make one, you can use 'embroidery paste'. It is a kind of fabric paint (see below), which comes in a tube with a small pointed nozzle, and may be used on all fabrics except purely synthetic ones, such as nylon. You sketch out the pattern on the fabric then squeeze out the paint to create the design. It has to be left to dry for several hours (obviously if you are creating a design using more than one colour, each has to be left to dry before the next can be applied), and when it is dry it has to be ironed on the reverse side. When it is dry it gives the appearance of embroidery. It is washable, colour fast up to 60° centigrade, and

*You can achieve
stunning results with
embroidery paste or fabric paints*

available in black, white, red, blue, green, pink, yellow and brown.

'Ethnic' clothes

If you want to create a sensation and wear something really glamorous for a special party, what about wearing a sari, or a pair of tight trousers and a colourful robe of the type Pakistani ladies wear, or even a bold African print? These clothes usually come in gorgeous fabrics and glowing colours, and if you don't fancy the bare midriff of a sari in cool weather you could wear a body stocking underneath. You can buy these clothes in special shops in the more cosmopolitan quarters of town, and they need not be terribly expensive.

Fabric painting

You can buy special fabric paints and pens to create beautiful designs and motifs on plain fabrics. They can be used on almost all fabrics except silk and totally synthetic ones such as nylon. The design can be simply painted on, or transferred using an iron-on transfer. This leaves a permanent outline, so it has to be painted over.

The paint comes in small pots and is applied with a small brush. The fabric is stretched out and pinned to a firm base, and paper inserted between the layers of fabric (e.g. between the back and front of a T-shirt) to stop the paint seeping through. Once the paint is absolutely dry (and this can take up to twenty-four hours) the design is ironed on the reverse side for a few minutes, after which it becomes permanent, and is washable.

Fabric paints can also be used to enhance an existing design. For example, if you have a floral pattern, you can pick out certain flowers with the paint, giving a solid, three-dimensional effect to the design, which looks terrific.

Fabric pens are used in a similar way, and are ideal for writing witty messages on T-shirts, for example. Both paints and pens are available from art shops and come with full instructions. They are produced in a range of colours, including gold, silver and copper, and other colours with glitter effects.

Flowers

You may worry that people will think you are old-fashioned if you wear flowers, but don't believe it. For a special occasion, wear a real flower, such as a rose, either fixed to a slide in your hair, pinned to the front of your dress or jacket, or tucked into the bosom of a low neckline. It always looks terribly romantic and pretty. If it is winter time and fresh flowers are expensive, then buy one of the beautiful silk ones available and wear that instead.

Flowers also look fantastic on hats, and if you wear the right kind of clothes with them you will not look like a refugee from the Women's Institute.

Gloves

Once everyone wore them; then they were considered necessary only for wear in cold weather. But nowadays lots of people wear gloves for fun, and they are available in all kinds of colours and designs. A plain pair of gloves can be decorated with fabric paints, or with embroidery. A pretty pair of lace gloves can be made even more attractive by threading a piece of ribbon through each wristband. Small beads or sequins can also be sewn on gloves for a very pretty effect. With fabric paints you can create all kinds of bold designs, and could even paint each finger a different colour to create a rainbow effect, which would be gorgeous! Remember, if you do this you must let each colour dry properly before applying the next.

Gold and glitz

The designer Christian Lacroix has recently brought out a 'baroque' look, which consists of a layering of details and a heavily decorated appearance, encrusted with gold. It is very dramatic, and with a little effort and imagination can be created reasonably cheaply at home. The essence of the look is heavy gold jewellery, which can be created by sticking sequins on to broad bands of stiff ribbon, such as petersham, to make 'necklaces' which can then be sewn on to your clothes. You could also buy lengths of chain very cheaply from a plumber's or builder's merchant and spray them with gold glitter, or you could buy a brass (or imitation brass) door finger plate and wear it as a brooch or hang it from a chain to make a pendant. (The Lacroix models wore door knockers as brooches, but I think they must have found them rather heavy!)

Gold and glitz

You can use sequins to create little gold points on collars, too, and spray the heels of high-heeled shoes with gold paint. The glitz look will probably be a bit over the top for most people as daytime wear, but would be great for a special evening.

Hair

Ideas for brightening up your hairstyle are given in Chapter 8, but the purpose of including it here is to mention that your hair must be taken into account if you are trying to create a particular effect. If you are trying to look glamorous, your hair has to look special, too. Perhaps you could create a dramatic style with a hot styling brush, and then pin an ornament in your hair. On the other hand, if you are dressed in jeans and a sweatshirt, your hair would be best left to look casual, or you would just appear silly. So don't forget to include your hairstyle in your plans.

Improvisation

In a way, most of this book is about improvisation, which means doing something without preparation. For example, you may have been asked out somewhere special, or by someone special, and your only decent clothes may be at the cleaners. Don't refuse the invitation — improvise! Look back to Chapter 1 and all the things you could do with a bit of imagination. Even if you only have your jeans to wear, put on a well-cut shirt or a pretty blouse, do your hair attractively, wear some exciting jewellery, take care with your make-up — if you wear it — and add a dab of perfume, and you will look good enough to go to most places.

Jewellery

Jewellery, and how to make fun things simply and cheaply, is described on pages 88 to 97. As with the hair, jewellery should suit the clothes you are wearing and the occasion on which you are wearing it.

Knitting

This is also described elsewhere (pages 82 to 88), but is included here as a reminder. Lots of people think knitting is a fuddy-duddy pastime fit only for grannies to indulge in, whereas nothing could be farther from the truth. There are some stunning patterns for knitwear around nowadays, and if you can knit you can create some fabulous effects for a fraction of the price you would pay for the finished article in the shops. If you *can't* knit, perhaps now is a good time to learn!

Layers

Wearing what shops call 'separates' gives you an easy way of creating interesting effects. For example, you might wear a red T-shirt under a green shirt with a sweater, cardigan or jacket on

The layered look

top. But another time you could wear the T-shirt over the shirt, with or without the jumper, to give a different look. More glamorous fabrics can be layered, too. A shiny fabric in a strong colour can create a fascinating look worn under a semi-transparent top, or with a shawl or scarf swathed over it. As explained on page 10, blouses, jumpers and T-shirts can all be worn under sleeveless or short-sleeved dresses to create a particular effect, and large T-shirts, loose sweaters or men's shirts look great worn over tights, leggings or body stockings. So be inventive with your layers — they'll keep you warm as well as looking good.

Men's clothes

You may buy men's clothes because they fit you better than girls', because they can be turned into something entirely different from what the manufacturer intended, or simply because they are available in better colours in the men's department than in the women's, sweaters being a good example. Very large shirts and sweaters can be worn as dresses, held in at the waist with a belt. Men's ties can be worn with a shirt, or used as belts. Pyjamas may make attractive summer trouser suits with the sleeves and legs rolled up. You may even find that, if you have a largeish waist and smallish hips, men's jeans and trousers fit you better than women's. So it is worth keeping an eye on men's shops. If you feel embarrassed, you could always pretend to be buying a present for your brother.

Necessity

Necessity, says the proverb, is the mother of invention, and if you need something badly enough and apply your mind to it, I dare say you will achieve it! It won't bring you a million pounds to spend on your clothes, but it may well point out how you can change or adapt something to suit the occasion.

Odd socks, tights and sleeves

An amusing effect can be created by wearing two different coloured pairs of tights, with one leg cut out of each (there is usually a hole or a ladder in one leg and not the other, anyway) so you can go around with, for example, one blue leg and one green one. With socks it's easy, because you just wear one sock from one pair and one from another, but make sure they have something in common or it might look peculiar. For example, if you have one red pair of socks with white spots on them and one white pair with red spots on them you could wear one of each, but one thin white cotton sock and one ribbed navy wool sock would look a bit too odd!

To make odd sleeves, cut one sleeve off each of two T-shirts and sew them on to the other one, thus making two shirts with odd sleeves. Be careful with shirts, though, as sleeves which are 'set in' and which button at the cuff are right or left sleeves, and may not be interchangeable. Also check with your mum that you are allowed to go chopping sleeves off things – she may think it is all a dreadful waste of good clothing!

Paints for shoes

Shoes can be dyed, but it is easier and the results are often better if you paint them with special shoe paints. These can be bought in a variety of colours from shoe shops, shoe repair shops and haberdashery departments. As well as dyeing shoes exciting colours, shoe paints can be used to create stripes, spots and other designs, using more than one colour, as long as you remember to let one colour dry before applying the next. For a special party you could even stick bands of sequins on your shoes, or spread them with glue and shake glitter over them, or over the heels, to give a really stunning effect.

Quilting

Quilting simply means putting another layer of fabric behind the area of fabric you wish to quilt and putting padding between the two layers, to make a thickened and raised design. It is a good way of making part of a patterned fabric stand out. For example, if you had a floral patterned jacket, with lots of blue flowers on it and just the odd red one, you could quilt each of the red flowers and make them stand out even more. It also works well if you want to make an interesting looking bag. (For more details about quilting, see *Freaky Fashions*.)

Ribbons and braid

A browse through the haberdashery or furnishing fabrics department of a large store will produce a wealth of lovely ribbons and braids which can be used to revamp your clothes. Braid can be sewn round the hems of skirts or trousers, used to bind the cuffs of shirts and pockets, or used to make belts, hair ribbons, choker necklaces and bracelets. Furnishing fabrics trimmings often yield beautiful silky embroidered braids, which would make lovely belts, either used singly or with two or three pieces slip-stitched together to make a wider belt.

Braid decorates a skirt (right) or a belt (below)

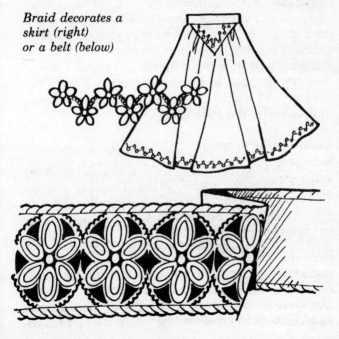

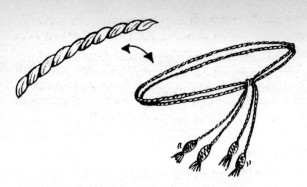

Similarly, the silky cords used to tie back curtains can make attractive belts, and may be used singly or twisted upon themselves to make wider ones.

Scarves

Scarves come in many different shapes and types, and can be used in a variety of ways. Forget the frumpy old headscarf or Sloane Ranger images, and consider the following:

Long woolly scarves

These look great worn with a chunky knitted jumper, or over a winter jacket. They can also be wrapped round your head for protection against the cold and rain. Buy or knit one in a bright colour to contrast cheerfully with your jacket, or in creamy Aran wool for a sumptuous effect.

Small squares

These can be tied, cowboy-fashion, round the neck to add colour to an otherwise plain, round-necked jumper or T-shirt, put into the pocket of a jacket or sweater, or worn around your head, either as a scarf or rolled into a band. If you have a number of different coloured small squares you can knot them together to make a sash belt for a plain dress. They can even be knotted together to make a bikini — but make sure the knots don't slip!

Large squares

These have a multitude of uses, so the more of them you can acquire, the better. Obviously you can wear one, Sloane-style, round your head. You can also knot one round your neck over a sweater to leave the long ends trailing, or tie two together to make a sash. If you buy two matching squares you can slip-stitch them together, as shown in the diagram, to make a tabard top which, in bright,

Tabard top

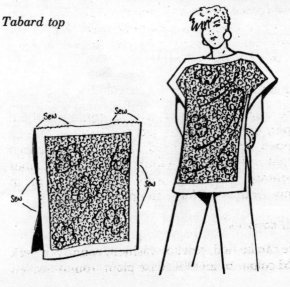

rich, silky colours, would look terrific over a black body stocking, or black T-shirt and tights or leggings. In a similar way, if you have several large squares and don't mind cutting them into rectangles, you could make a floaty overskirt to be worn over leggings.

Four large squares could even be turned into a slinky dress by slip-stitching them into place, and wearing a belt to hold it together.

Heavy real silk scarves can be expensive, but thin, light Indian silk ones can often be found quite cheaply, and synthetic fabrics can look almost, but not quite, as good. Large wool or wool mixture squares look good worn over a winter coat or jacket, or they make warm and elegant shawls. Jumble sales and secondhand shops can be a good source of scarves if the prices in the shops put you off. (See page 72 for a wonderful top that can be created from scarves.)

Sequins

Sequins can be bought in all colours, and look splendid sewn on party clothes, making them shimmer in the light. Paris couturiers have used them to adorn glittering waistcoats, or sewn them on to the collar of a dress or jacket. One particularly sophisticated and effective way to wear them is to sew black sequins on to the lapels of a plain black jacket. Or you could draw a pattern across the top and shoulder area of a dress, sweater, cardigan or blouse and sew sequins on to that. The kind of Prince of Wales feathers spray which was very popular in the 1940s is now coming back into

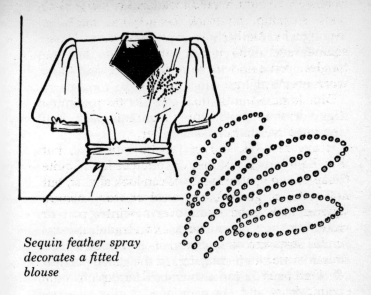

*Sequin feather spray
decorates a fitted
blouse*

fashion and could easily be created in this way. This pattern on a velvet or velour top would look stunning. Sequins are also useful for decorating belts and jewellery.

Shimmer

For a very special party, dab spots of adhesive on a T-shirt or other inexpensive piece of clothing and shake glitter (the kind used for Christmas decorations) all over it. It will stick to the glue and create a lovely shimmering effect. You could either do this all over the T-shirt, or make a pattern with the glue. A similar effect could be created using spray-on hair glitter. But don't use either of these methods on any clothes you want to keep in perfect condition, for you will never be able to get the glitter off entirely.

Shimmer can be created in other ways, too. You can buy make-up with shimmer effects, and sheer, shimmering tights, which look great for a party. Gold shimmering tights look good on suntanned legs, or you could dust your legs with gold shimmer eyeshadow instead.

Socks

Fabric paint can be used to create amusing patterns round the tops of your socks. You could make coloured stripes, a daisy chain, or, if you felt artistic, a border of kittens playing, or a big, red, double-decker bus. You can also embroider designs on to your socks, and, as mentioned earlier, wearing odd socks – e.g. one red and one blue – can be very effective.

Tie-dyeing

Tie-dyeing consists of tying fabric in certain places and immersing it in dye. The dye will not penetrate the tied areas, so when the cloth is dry and unrolled you are left with a white (or whatever colour it was to start with) pattern on it. You can then tie the fabric differently and immerse it in another colour, to get a different effect. Tie-dyeing is a good way of livening up plain cotton summer clothes. (For more details on tie-dying see *Freaky Fashions*.)

Trompe l'oeil

Trompe l'oeil means 'deceive the eye', and this idea can be used in a variety of ways to make amusing clothes. For example, on a plain sweater you can sew a row of beads to look like a separate necklace, or embroider (or paint on with a fabric pen) a collar and tie, a pair of braces, and so on. You could even

Eye deceivers: the trompe l'oeil look

create *trompe l'oeil* tears in clothes to give a punk effect. For example, if you wore a coloured T-shirt under another shirt you could make 'slashes' on the top garment with a fabric pen the same colour as the garment underneath, so it would look as if the T-shirt was showing through the tears. Rings can be embroidered or painted on gloves, a belt on a dress, a bracelet on a sweater, and so on.

Underwear

Although it isn't seen much, wearing the right underwear on the right occasion will make you feel better, and as we have seen, if you feel right you will look right.

Under tight-fitting clothes, snugly-fitting briefs and an almost seamless bra are best, as they don't show unsightly lines and wrinkles. But if you are dressing up for a special occasion and fancy a bit of glamour you might like to invest in a slinky camisole top and matching French knickers in a colour to match your dress. You could always ask for them for a Christmas or birthday present if funds are short.

Existing underwear can be transformed by dyeing it, especially if it was once white and has become a dirty greyish colour. Follow the manufacturer's instructions, and dye your underclothes a stunning colour, such as peacock blue, bright pink, emerald green or violet, to cheer you up when you put them on in the morning.

Velvet and velour

These luxury fabrics look wonderful on special occasions. One way of acquiring a velvet dress or skirt more cheaply than buying it from a shop is to make it. You will probably find that the furnishing fabrics department of a store has a better choice of colours and is cheaper than the dress fabrics department.

You can also buy shiny velvet, called panne velvet, which looks wonderful for a party dress, and is sometimes available in stunning patterns as well as plain colours.

White

Some people discount white when planning their clothes, but it can look very good indeed. It looks wonderful with dark skin or a tan, but a softly romantic summer dress would look equally good with a pale skin and white tights. You can create a totally different effect by wearing it with black — here you will look dramatic. To be effective, however, white *must* be sparkling clean — it's no use expecting to wear a white shirt more than once before washing. If you wear white shoes, keep these clean, too, or the effect is very depressing. If you are not prepared to spend time keeping your white clothes clean, then it is better not to buy any.

eXcitement

Excitement in the way we dress is what this book is all about. It may be achieved by wearing bright and cheerful colours, a daringly short mini skirt, a low-cut dress, a dramatic hair style or colour, imaginative make-up (such as that shown on pages 105 to 113), or clever ornamentation, such as the door-chain belt on page 98. One or two exciting extras are enough, however. Put them all together and you risk one cancelling out the effect of the others.

Yellow

Depending on how you look at it, yellow is either a bright, cheerful, spring-like colour, or a biliously unattractive one, which makes everything it comes into contact with look awful. If you have read the chapter on colour, you will realize that the way you view it depends on your own skin colouring. Those with golden-toned skins look good in yellow; those with blue-toned skins don't. Having said that, there may well be a *shade* of yellow that you can wear, in the range from lemon to mustard. Or, if you like the colour but feel it doesn't complement your skin tone, then don't wear it next to your face. Instead of wearing a yellow sweater, wear a yellow belt or a pair of yellow shoes (guaranteed to catch the eye), which will give the cheerful effect without making you look ill.

pZazz!

Pzazz is what you need to be a leader of fashion. You have to be daring and adventurous, and not afraid of starting a trend, or appearing different from your friends. A lot of this is a matter of self-confidence, and to gain self-confidence it helps to know that you look right. So spend time planning your looks, and when you're sure you've got it right, go out and conquer the world!

5. Creating a Look

You may feel that you want to create a specific 'look' with your clothes, that defines you as a certain type of person. This look may be total, in that you always wear the kind of clothes that create it, or it may be that you prefer to opt for different looks at different times, according to the occasion or how you feel. Either way, the easiest method of achieving it is to study the people whose clothes produce the effect for which you are aiming. If necessary go around with a notebook and pencil and write down what they are wearing! Analyse what goes into the look and see if you can reproduce it with the clothes you already own, or, if not, what you need to buy in order to do so. It may be that you can manage with just an accessory or two to add the finishing authentic touch. Don't forget when doing your research to note the person's hairstyle and make-up, if applicable. It is these kinds of details that make all the difference between getting it just right and looking somehow unfinished. Below are some of the looks you can create, and how to achieve them.

*

The Pretty Look

The pretty look harks back to the past, when girls wore long dresses, had long hair, and were expected to behave in a ladylike fashion. Nowadays it tends to mean longish, flowing dresses in soft, pastel colours; long hair, elegantly put up or worn as flowing curls; delicate, rather than exciting make-up; and a touch of light floral scent, or even lavender water.

Dresses and skirts don't necessarily have to sweep the floor or be Victorian in style. The clothes ladies wore in the 1920s, pre-flapper style, low-waisted, mid-calf length, and worn with a long matching jacket, would be ideal. The colours should be pale and soft — white, cream, pastels — and the clothes should be worn with matching pale tights and shoes, and, if possible, a hat. A pair of lace gloves would complete the picture.

If you don't feel you can go to all that trouble and expense (though you could collect the various components bit by bit), you could still achieve a pretty effect with a long, flowing skirt and a pretty blouse, possibly lace-trimmed (you could add the lace to an existing blouse yourself). A brooch at the throat, your hair pinned up with a comb or a flower in it, and possibly small, delicate earrings, would complete the look.

In winter you could wear a velvet skirt with a blouse as described above, and to make it a bit warmer, wear a tapestry waistcoat, velvet jacket, or a shawl over the top. You could also wear warm thick tights, if they matched your skirt, and little button-up ankle boots with small heels. For this

The pretty look

look, your shoes should always have little heels rather than being high-heeled or flat.

If you like wearing trousers, you could try a masculine/feminine look. Wear a pair of velvet knickerbockers with dark tights, a frilled shirt with a pretty scarf tied in a floppy bow at the neck, a shiny waistcoat or jacket and a long cloak.

*The masculine/
feminine look*

Regency-style chunky shoes with a buckle on the front would go well with these clothes.

If you feel really happy with this look, it is also worthwhile investing in pretty underwear to complement it. Again you can sew on lace or little bows of silk ribbon yourself, to avoid having to spend lots of money on beautiful underwear.

The Streetwise Look

This is about as far away as you can get from the pretty look. It is utilitarian, and can look downright aggressive. It means wearing jeans and leather jackets, and having a short, unisex hairstyle, fluffed up or gelled into spikes. The only ornamentation is likely to be a pair of large earrings, and motorbike-type studs on the jacket.

Most people own a pair of jeans, so that part of the look is readily available. If you like to carry things to extremes, you may like to wear jeans with holes or tears in them, or even make them specially, though this is unlikely to be popular with your parents.

With the jeans, wear a white T-shirt (low-necked if you want to look sexy), and a short denim or leather jacket. The latter are very expensive, but if you keep your eyes open you may well find quite a good imitation leather jacket at a reasonable price. It may also square with your conscience better, too, if you dislike the thought of wearing animal skins.

Studs for fixing to the jacket can be bought cheaply at bikers' shops and sewn, glued or riveted in position.

For decoration, you could wear a punk-style chain belt (which you can buy cheaply as a length of chain from a builder's merchant), and large dangly earrings, which can be bought inexpensively in most chain stores.

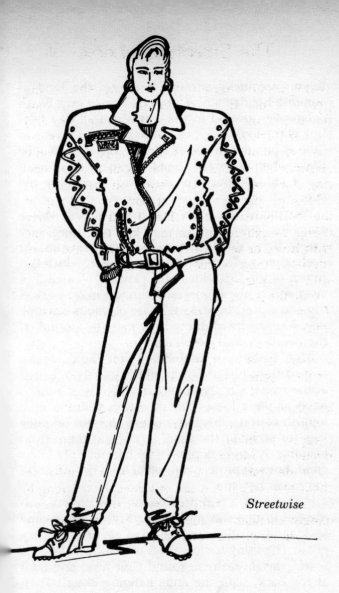

Streetwise

The Summer Holiday Look

If you are lucky enough to go on the kind of summer holiday where you can lounge on a beach or wander around in the warm sun all day then this is the look for you. You will want to wear as little as possible in such a climate, but there will be times when you need something to cover yourself up, if only to stop your skin from burning in the sun.

You might like to buy a cotton bikini with a matching skirt and top, which can look very pretty. If you don't like the idea of exposing all that flesh, then go for the latest beachwear, which is a return of the 1950s idea of a 'playsuit' — a kind of swimsuit-cum-mini-dress, with a scoop-necked top and a short frilly skirt. These playsuits can look very pretty, and most can be worn to lie around on the beach as well as to swim in.

After bathing or sunbathing you could wear a large cotton shirt or T-shirt, either loosely or belted at the waist. Until you get tanned, it is as well to have either a loose pair of cotton trousers or a longish cotton skirt, too, to keep the sun off your legs for some of the time, to prevent them from burning. A large, floppy straw hat not only looks good, but will protect your head from the effects of too much hot sun.

Hair can be a real problem on this type of holiday. If it gets wet in the sea it tends to become sticky and unruly when dry, and never looks very good. The thing to do with it is to hide it. Wrap a scarf, peasant-fashion, round your head and tie it at the back, with the ends hanging down. Then

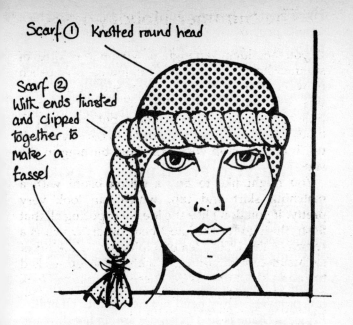

Scarf ① Knotted round head

Scarf ② With ends twisted and clipped together to make a tassel

roll another, contrasting scarf, into a tube. Tie this round your head along the edge of the first, and twist its loose ends round and hold them in place with little gold-coloured clips, or bits of wire, to make a fetching tassel. You can then go happily from the beach to shop in the town, to eat in a restaurant, or even to dance in a disco, without having to wash and style your hair.

Once you have a tan, you can wear all kinds of terrific looking clothes. A low-backed dress looks great, as do mini-skirts, cropped tops, and tops with pieces cut out of them to reveal the tanned skin beneath. Choose pale colours to look cool, blue and white stripes to look cool and sporty, or vivid shades like lime, fuchsia and orange, which would probably be unwearable with a pale skin, but which look super with a darker one.

No summer holiday look would be complete without sunglasses. There are so many styles to choose from that you may be bewildered, but make sure when you buy a pair that they are comfortable and feel right, as well as looking right.

The Winter Glamour Look

The secret of looking good in our climate in winter is to wear enough clothes to feel warm. You cannot look attractive if you scurry around in a thin dress, shivering and blue with cold, pulling a face as you clutch your jacket to yourself.

One of the best ways of keeping warm is to wear lots of layers. They need not necessarily be bulky. Princess Diana is said to keep warm in her thin and elegant dresses by wearing thermal underwear underneath! If you don't like the idea of thermal underwear, then at least wear a cotton vest, and if you can't even bear the idea of that, then wear a T-shirt under all your clothes.

Winter clothes can look terrific. Either wear a long skirt with matching thick tights, with a shirt, sweater and even a waistcoat on top, or wear your favourite mini, with thick ribbed tights or leggings. Boots are a must, and have the added advantage that you can wear an extra pair of socks underneath them, to keep your feet even warmer. Over all this, wear a long topcoat, or a hip-length jacket, and wind a long woolly scarf round your neck, leaving the ends free to blow in the wind.

Winter glamour: bright colours and lots of layers

Hats add the finishing touch and keep you much warmer, too, for we lose much of our body heat through our uncovered heads in cold weather.

Bright colours and bright make-up look good on dreary winter days, and will make you look especially attractive. You can add colour with your hat, scarf and woolly gloves, which could, for example, have a different colour for each finger, or an amusing pattern sewn on to their backs.

For a sporting winter look, wear trousers and
boots, with layers of thick and thin jumpers, such
as a thin polo neck under a heavy Guernsey or
Icelandic-style sweater, and a warm jacket. A
brightly coloured beret and scarf look good with
this outfit.

You could also go in for the Russian fur look, with a fur-trimmed long coat, long boots, a muff and a cossack hat. Most caring people nowadays don't wear real fur, even if they can afford it, knowing the horrors undergone by the animals involved, but you can buy 'fun' furs made from special fabrics, either in the form of jackets and coats, or by the metre, to sew as a trimming round a collar, for example.

The Disco Look

When it comes to discos, almost anything goes. If you are feeling casual, you might want to wear your jeans and a T-shirt. You may want to leap around in your shortest, tightest skirt, with a pair of white ankle socks and your Doc Martens. You may want to wear a Smiley top and a pair of leggings, or you may want to dress up in all the glitter and glamour you can find. A lot depends on where you live and the kind of discos you go to.

One way of producing most of these looks with the minimum of clothing and expenditure is to buy a short cotton jersey dress, with a low back or front. This can be worn either way round to make it look different. If it has sleeves, you could roll them up to elbow length and wear gauntlets over your lower arms, made from the legs of black fishnet tights, with sequins sewn on to them. You could buy a piece of satiny fabric in a contrasting colour and make a wide sash to tie in a huge bow at the back, or buy a number of ready-made bows and sew them down the back (or the front,

The disco look

depending on which way round you wear the dress) from the low neck. If it is a black dress, you could buy a wide black belt, and stick bikers' studs on it so it looks like a giant bulldog's collar, wear a chain round your neck and black gloves, and you will look really sinister! You could wear the dress over leggings or tights in a contrasting colour, or just go for glamour with shiny tights, big earrings and high-heeled shoes.

If it's a glitzy look you're after, you could go in for the gold and glitter effect. Wear a very short, tight, black mini skirt with a skimpy lurex vest top together with black tights and black high-heeled shoes, with the heels sprayed gold. Or wear a black dress with a short full skirt and a net petticoat underneath — showing slightly — with a gold lurex sash round the middle, and a heavy gold necklace and earrings. Or wear a body stocking, or T-shirt and matching opaque tights, with a fringed 'skirt' over the top, which will spin around amazingly as you dance. Or you could even go to the opposite extreme, and wear a short-skirted suit with a fitted jacket, with, daringly, no shirt beneath it.

The Way Out Look

If almost anything goes with the disco look, then anything at all goes with the way out look. You need a bit of courage to wear it — it certainly isn't for shrinking violets — but if you can summon the courage, you will be rewarded by being the most stunning dresser around.

*Way
Out*

If you are a way out kind of person, then you probably have lots of ideas yourself for this sort of look, but if you are just aspiring to it, here are some suggestions.

Wear a bustier over a dress, or even over a body stocking. Wear a low-necked dress over a brightly coloured vest, with matching tights or leggings. Wear a mini skirt or dress over a long, see-through skirt or petticoat. Wear a summer sundress or beach suit over bright red tights with a matching polo neck jumper. In winter, wear your summer shorts over two pairs of tights of different colours, so you have one red leg and one green one, with a striped jersey of matching colours. Wear one of your summer dresses with a cut-out neck, or other cut-out pieces, over a brightly-coloured body stocking and tights. For a party, make a very full, flounced skirt, and wear it with a cropped T-shirt top.

There are lots of ideas throughout the book for daring accessories, but don't forget that if you want to look really different, you must invest in some kind of exotic hairstyle. If you can't do anything with your hair, then save up and buy a wig, even if it is the synthetic variety. Then you can make it stand on end, spray coloured streaks into it, perm it, or do anything you like with it, without affecting your real hair and having to put up with the consequences.

6. Make Your Own

Scarf Top

Materials and measurements

Six 35cm square scarves will fit up to 76cm bust.
Six 40cm square scarves will fit up to 96cm bust.
Length from centre back neck will be 35 or 40cm
    depending on size of scarves.

If you can't find scarves the right size, just cut
squares to the appropriate size and neaten the
edges with as narrow a hem as possible. It is more
interesting to use scarves with different but com-
plementing colours and patterns, but the weight of
cloth must be similar.

To complete

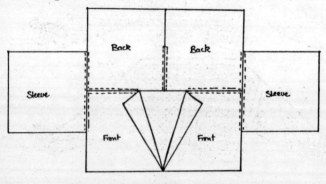

1. Lay the squares as shown in the diagram on page 72 and, with right sides together, stitch as shown along the dotted lines. Leave open 8cm of each side of the centre back.

2. With the right sides together, stitch the under-arm seams as shown.

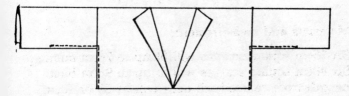

3. Roll back the cuffs to the required length and tie each side of the sleeve together with a small knot. Backs and fronts can also be joined with small knots.

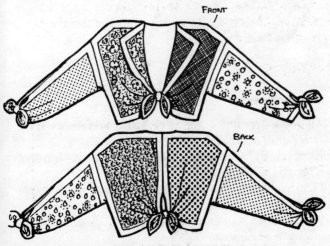

Handkerchief Skirt

No, this isn't made out of old handkerchiefs (ugh!). A handkerchief skirt is one in which the hem is not straight, but forms a series of points.

Measurements

All measurements are very approximate as they depend on fabric width.

90cm cloth – shortest length is 45cm, longest length is 65cm.

112cm cloth – shortest length is 55cm, longest length is 77cm.

150cm cloth – shortest length is 75cm, longest length is 105cm.

Materials

110cm fabric on 90cm cloth, or
130cm fabric on 112cm cloth, or
170cm fabric on 150cm cloth.
Waist length piece of 2cm wide elastic (see
  pattern).

Sums first

1. Measure your waist in centimetres. Then
subtract 5cm. This figure is called A, and is the
amount of elastic you will need.

2. Measure your hips in centimetres. Then add
10cm. This figure is called B.

3. Divide B by 6.25 (using a calculator!) Then
subtract 1cm. The total is called C, and will be
needed later on.

To cut out the skirt

1. Fold the fabric from point E to point D as shown
to make the square skirt. Cut along the fabric from
G to D.

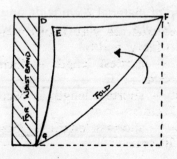

2. Fold the fabric from point F to point G and mark H which is the centre of the skirt.

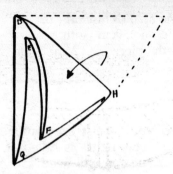

3. Measure and mark measurement C from point H as shown. Cut along this line for the hipline. Now hem the four straight edges of the skirt.

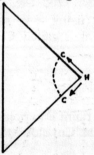

4. Cut a strip of material 20cm wide and measurement B in length, as shown. This will be the waist-band.

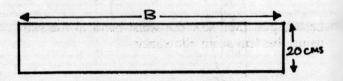

5. Join the ends of the waist-band with a 1cm seam. Cut the elastic to A cm, and stick the elastic together by overlapping the ends to make a circle.

6. Fold a 35mm turning over at the top of the waist-band and, while enclosing the elastic, stitch around the band using a 1cm seam allowance. But be careful not to stitch through the elastic!

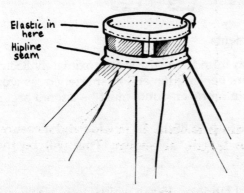

Elastic in here

Hipline seam

Lastly, pin, then sew the waist-band to the skirt using the 1cm seam allowance.

Turkish Trousers

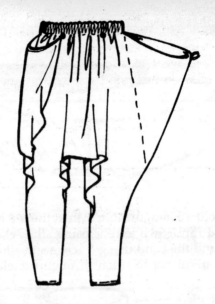

Measurements

The length from the waist is approximately 85cm.
This can be lengthened or shortened as you
wish, but fabric amounts must be altered accor-
dingly.
To fit waist up to 85cm.

Materials

2 metres of fabric on 150cm width cloth. Use a soft
silky or knitted type of fabric which will drape
well.
Waist length piece of 3cm wide elastic (see
pattern).

To make trouser pattern

Using a large piece of paper, plot out the points marked with crosses as shown on the diagram, following the measurements given.

If you want to add or subtract length to your trousers, do this now!

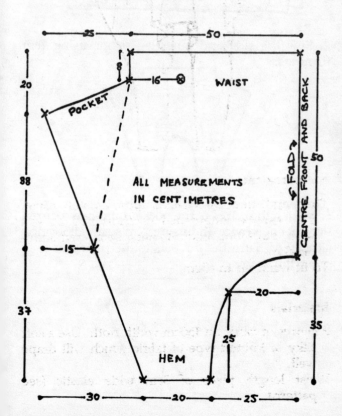

Trouser Pattern

POCKET

WAIST

CENTRE FRONT AND BACK

FOLD

ALL MEASUREMENTS IN CENTIMETRES

HEM

To make the trousers

1. Cut out the pattern and lay it on the fabric as shown.

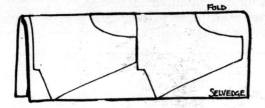

2. Sew the side and inner leg seams using 1cm turnings.

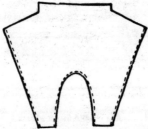

3. Neaten the edges of the pockets and hems, turning the edge twice and using 2cm seam allowance altogether. Turn the trousers to the right side and press the seams.

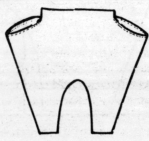

4. Lay the trousers flat and mark a line for pockets with pins through the trouser legs. Stitch.

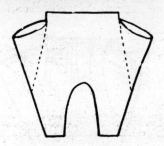

5. Measure the elastic to waist measurement and deduct 5cm. Cut the elastic to this length and stitch with a flat seam by overlapping the ends.

6. Stitch up the remaining 10cm at each side of the waist-band.

7. Turn over 5cm at the top to the wrong side and, while enclosing the elastic, stitch 4cm from the fold. But be careful that you don't stitch through the elastic!

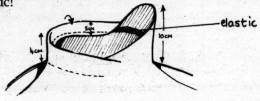

8. To finish off, a button can be added at about 15cm from each side seam and stitched just below the elastic. Make a loop with cotton, large enough to go over the button, at the seam on the pocket.

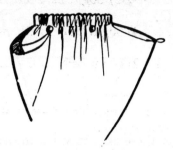

Jumper and Skirt with French-knitted Squiggles

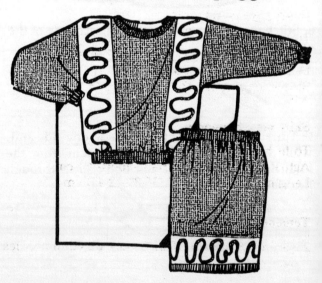

Materials

Jumper: 6 (6-7-7-7) 50gm balls in Double Knitting
  (DK) in main colour (A)
Jumper: 1 (2-2-2-2) 50gm balls in DK in contrast
  colour (B)
Skirt: 3 (2-3-4-4) 50gm balls in DK in main colour
  (A)
Skirt: 1 (1-1-1-2) 50gm balls in DK in contrast colour (B)
Waist-length piece of 2mm wide elastic
1 pair each of 3¼mm and 4mm knitting needles
1 french-knitting nancy
1 crochet hook
2 stitch-holders
Amounts of yarn are based on average require-
  ments and are therefore approximate.

Jumper measurements

To fit chest/bust size: 71 (76-81-86-91) cm
Actual measurement: 76 (81-86-91-96) cm
Length: 43 (46-49-52-55) cm
Sleeve length: 42 (43-44-45-46) cm

Skirt measurements

To fit hip size: 71 (76-81-86-91) cm
Actual measurement: 76 (81-86-91-96) cm
Length: (adjustable) 33 (36-39-42-45) cm

Tension

23sts and 29 rows to 10cm square on 4mm needles
  over st st.

Abbreviations

k=knit; p=purl; st(s)=stitch(es); st st=stocking stitch; rev st st=reverse stocking stitch; beg=beginning; foll=following; inc=increase; dec=decrease; cont=continue; WS=wrong side; rep=repeat; alt=alternate; rem=remaining; cm=centimetres; A=main colour; B=rib colour; RSF=right side facing.

French-knitting

1. Using A, and a French-knitting nancy, thread the end of the yarn through the nancy, then wind the long end of the yarn around the four loops as shown.

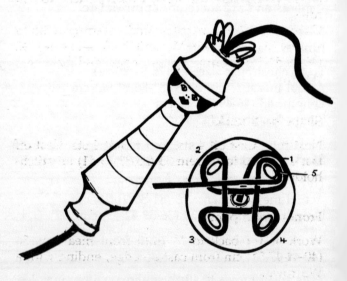

2. Wrap the first loop again but this time lift the first stitch over the top of the loop with the crochet hook, making sure that the fifth stitch, just formed, stays on the loop. Continue working new stitches around the nancy but as you work pull the thread at the bottom of the nancy to keep the stitches even. Cut the thread and cast off when knitting measures approximately 4 metres.

You will need two 4-metre lengths for the jumper and one 4-metre length for the skirt.

Back (centre panel)

With 3¼mm needles and A, cast on 41 (43-45-47-49) sts and work in k1*p1 k1* for 10 rows.
Change to 4mm needles and, starting with a k row, work in st st** until back measures 43 (46-49-52-55) cm from cast-on edge, ending with a WS row.

Shape back neck

Next row: Cast off 4 sts, knit to last 4 sts. Cast off last 4 sts and leave rem 33 (35-37-39-41) on stitch-holder.

Front (centre panel)

Work as for back to ** until front measures 36 (40-44-47-51) cm from cast-on edge, ending with a WS row.

Shape front neck

Next row: k10, slip next 21 (23-25-27-29) sts on to stitch-holder, turn and ***dec 1st at neck edge on every row until 4 sts remain. Cont straight in st st until front measures the same as back from cast-off edge, ending with a WS row. Cast off.

Rejoin yarn to rem 10 sts and k to end of row. Now work as for first side from *** to end.

Side panels (make 2)

With 3¼mm needles and A, cast on 25 (27-29-31-33) sts and work in k1*p1 k1* for 10 rows.

Change to 4mm needles and B, and starting with a p row, work in rev st st until panel measures 43 (46-49-52-55) cm from cast-on edge. Using contrast yarn mark each end of row for shoulder line.

Cont as before until panel measures 82.5 (88.5-94.5-100.5-106.5) cm from cast-on edge ending with WS row. Change to 3¼mm needles and A, and work in k1*p1 k1* for 10 rows. Cast off.

Sleeves

With 3¼mm needles and A, cast on 44 sts and work in *k1 p1* for 14 rows.

Change to 4mm needles.

Inc row: k4, inc in next st *k1, inc in next st rep from * to last 5 sts k (62 sts).

Now starting with a p row, work in st st inc 1 st at each end of every foll 6th rows until there are 92 (92-92-98-98) sts. Cont straight in st st until sleeve measures 42 (43-44-45-46) cm from cast-on edge ending with WS row. Cast off loosely.

Neckband

Join right shoulder.
With 3¼mm needles and A, with RSF pick up and k16 (16-14-12-12) sts down left front neck, K21 (23-25-27-29) sts from stitch-holder, K16 (16-14-12-12) sts up right neck front, and finally k33 (35-37-39-41) sts from back stitch-holder. (86[90-90-90-94] sts)
Work in *k1 p1* for 12 rows. Cast off ribwise fairly loosely.

To complete

Carefully press pieces on wrong side according to instructions given on the wrapper of your ball of wool (called the *ball-band instructions*).
Pin, then stitch french-knitting 'squiggles' into a curvy pattern as in picture.
Join left shoulder, then seam side panels to front and back.
Turn neckband to inside and slipstitch neatly but loosely.
Measure and mark 42 (42-42-44-44) cm each side of shoulder line and sew sleeves between these marks.
Join side and sleeve seams.

Front skirt

With 3¼mm needles and A, cast on 89 (95-101-107-113) sts and work in k1*p1 k1* for 10 rows.
Change to 4mm needles and B and starting with a p row cont in rev st st for 30 (32-34-36-38) rows.
Change to A and starting with a k row cont in st st until skirt measures 33 (36-39-42-45) cm from cast-on edge ending with WS row.

P for 2 rows then st st for 4 rows. Repeat last 6 rows once more. Cast off.
Work back skirt exactly as for front skirt.

To complete

Carefully press pieces on wrong side according to ball-band instructions.
Join one side seam, then pin and stitch french-knitting 'squiggles' into a curvy pattern as for jumper on to contrast panel.
Join rem side seam.
Measure waist in cm, subtract 5cm, and cut elastic to this length, overlapping ends, stitch elastic together. Now turn waistband over and insert elastic as you stitch along the waistline.

Jewel Box

Although you may admire Elizabeth Taylor's diamonds, you are fairly unlikely ever to be able to afford the real thing. But you can make very attractive jewellery without using jewels. Here are some ideas for you to try, or to adapt to suit yourself. Many of the materials can be used equally well to make other types of jewellery than that suggested. For example, material suitable for a necklace would work just as well with a belt or a hairband, while that suggested for rings would make equally good earrings.

Using 'blanks'

Craft shops, and shops that sell special stones and minerals, usually also sell jewellery 'blanks', which are the bases for many items you can make yourself. They include bases for rings, with adjustable hoops to fit any finger, bases for brooches, with a pin attached, small decorative fixing caps which can be strung on a thread and from which beads, etc. can be hung, and bases for earrings, which include the hoop that attaches to the ear as well as the part from which the decoration may be hung, or to which it may be attached. This type of shop also sells fastenings for necklaces, bracelets, and so on.

Some of the ideas below use jewellery blanks, but the general idea is to glue small stones, beads, and so forth, on to them. Natural things, like shells, seeds and feathers, can make very pretty jewellery, and it costs next to nothing to make.

Natural jewellery

Acorns

Collect the acorns in autumn when they are ripe, and paint them with clear varnish. (Colourless nail varnish would do.) You can leave them like this, or you may like to add a touch of gold by letting the varnish dry, and then dabbing small spots of adhesive around the upper part of each acorn and sprinkling gold glitter on it. Don't worry too much about getting an identical effect with each acorn, as the result will probably be prettier if they are slightly different. When this has dried, glue little gold-coloured fixing caps to their ends, and then string them on a thick gold thread (the sort used

*Acorn necklace, earring
and bracelet*

for wrapping presents would look nice), knotting
the thread round each loop to space them out
evenly. The ends of the thread can be tied to
fastening clips, or left long enough to tie at the
back of your neck. A bracelet can be made in a
similar way, and strung on rounded elastic to
avoid the need for a fastening. Acorns can also be
used to make earrings.

Shells
Long shells, such as mussel shells, and those little
spiral ones you find on beaches, can also be clear-
varnished (or if they are rather colourless,
varnished with pale pink pearly nail varnish) and
used in a similar way to the acorns above. Small
shells look pretty glued on to brooch blanks, or on
to hair bands, combs and slides. They also make

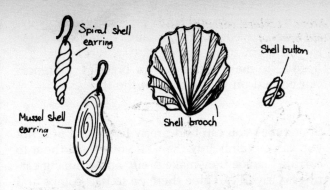

Spiral shell earring

Mussel shell earring

Shell brooch

Shell button

very pretty buttons glued on to blanks that have a loop for sewing through. Larger shells make attractive brooches, or can be glued on to a fixing cap through which a chain can be threaded to make a pendant.

Small stones
You may have noticed how pretty stones look when wet. If painted with clear varnish they retain their lovely sheen and can be used as described above. A single, prettily marked stone — say with a stripe or other marking — makes a most attractive brooch or ring when glued to an appropriate blank.

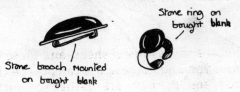

Stone ring on bought blank

Stone brooch mounted on bought blank

Seeds and pips
The idea of making jewellery from seeds and pips may sound bizarre, but it can be extremely effec-

tive. Melon seeds and apple pips make very pretty summer jewellery. Clean and dry them, then thread them on to strong button thread using a needle, to make a necklace or bracelet. Fasteners can be tied on to the ends of the thread.

Feathers
Sometimes you can find pretty feathers, but if not you can certainly buy them. If you attach them to earring blanks, they make pretty and amusing earrings. Or you can glue them on to hair combs and bands. You could even follow the Edwardian style by putting up your hair, if it is long enough, and

Feather hair ornaments

wearing a large feather in it, attached to a 'jewelled' comb, which can be made by sticking small coloured beads on to an ordinary hair comb.

Other simple jewellery

Wire

Picture wire, in gold or silver, or even ordinary fuse wire (13- or 30-amp) can be used to make most attractive jewellery. It can be coiled into flat spirals or cones to make earrings, coiled to make a necklace, bracelet or brooch, and twisted into delicate and pretty rings. You may like to thread small beads or stones on the wire coils for a more decorative effect.

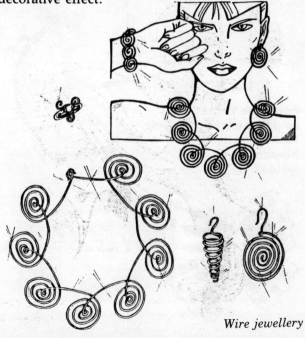

Wire jewellery

Paper or metal foil

These can be used to create lots of charming effects, though they have to be handled with care. One idea is to make small paper or foil cubes, as shown in the diagram, and then thread them on to button thread to make a necklace, or round elastic to make a bracelet.

Another idea is to trace the butterfly shape in the diagram on to a piece of thin cardboard, and cut it out. You may need to ask someone to help cut out

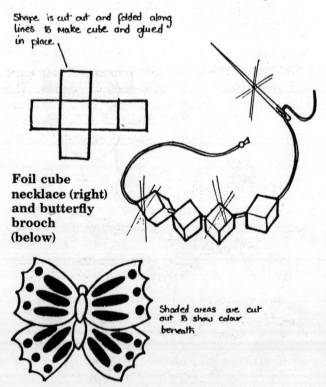

Shape is cut out and folded along lines to make cube and glued in place

Foil cube necklace (right) and butterfly brooch (below)

Shaded areas are cut out to show colour beneath

the delicate shapes with a craft knife. Spread adhesive over the cardboard butterfly and lay a piece of kitchen foil, or coloured paper, over the top. Press it down to stick it in place, and carefully cut round it, including the bits cut out of the wings. When it has dried, spread adhesive over the back of the cardboard and press that down on to a sheet of pretty coloured paper – one with a swirly pattern of different colours would be best. Cut that out round the edge only, so the colours show through. Tape a safety pin on to the back and you have a most attractive brooch.

Drinking straws
Carefully cut the straws into 1cm and 2cm lengths and then paint them with metallic paints. The easiest way to do this is to rig up a miniature washing line and string them on it, so you can paint them evenly all the way round. When they

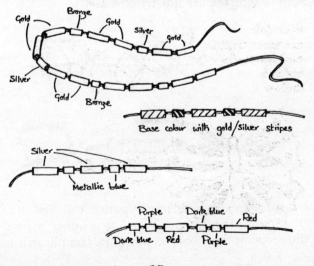

are dry, they can be strung on a thread to make a necklace or bracelet. If you want to vary the shape, add a small bead between each piece, or between every two pieces. If you put larger beads at the end, this will enable you to tie a knot to prevent the straws falling off the thread. Macaroni could be used in place of drinking straws to create the same effect.

Beads
Beads can be bought in all shapes and sizes from craft shops, and wonderful jewellery can be created from them. You can use glass beads in graded sizes to make a single strand for a necklace, or use beads all the same size and make a very long strand which can be wound round and round your neck.

Attractive chokers can be made by selecting wooden beads and mixing them with glass ones. Some examples are illustrated here.

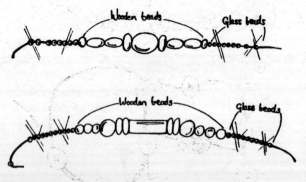

Beads can also be strung in patterns or woven to create stunning designs. Weaving is rather beyond the scope of this book, as it is quite complicated to do, but a form of stringing to make a series of flowers, which can be made into a necklace, bracelet, or belt, is illustrated below and on page 98.

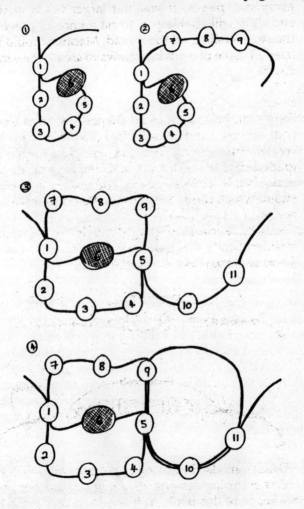

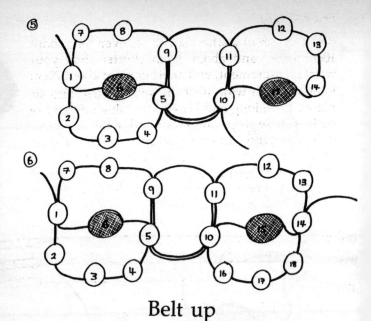

Belt up

Door chain belt

An amusing belt can be made with a length of chain bought from a hardware shop and the kind of door catch that has a sliding stop and chain. You may need to help to assemble it, for you will need to attach the chain to the screwholes of the catch, though this could be done with split rings or even tied with small pieces of wire. Wear the belt either tight round your waist, or slung loosely round your hips.

Fringed belt

Buy a length of leather, suede, or even felt, about 10cm wide, and about 10cm shorter than your waist measurement, and another piece about 20cm long and 8cm wide. Cut the second strip into six pieces 20cm long and 1cm wide. Glue one end of each of these strips on to each end of the first piece of leather, and thread a wooden or glass bead on to each free end. Tie a knot in each free end to stop the beads slipping off. To keep the belt in place when you wear it, simply knot the two lots of fringed ends together.

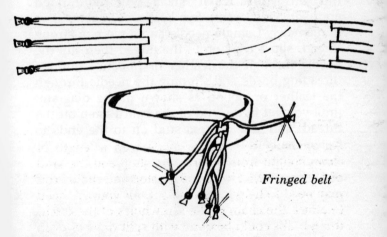

Fringed belt

Beaded belt

This belt can be made with leather and wooden beads, or with ribbon and glass beads in lovely colours, such as a deep wine red, silver grey, or a rich brown and gold. Cut a length of leather or ribbon, long enough to go round your waist, plus

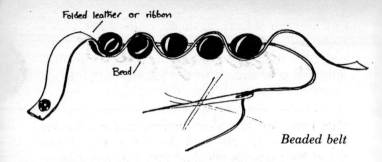

Folded leather or ribbon

Bead

Beaded belt

half as long again, and about 2cm wide. Depending on your waist size, you will need
approximately twenty-five beads, each about 1cm
in diameter. Using a needle and a piece of strong
thread, slip a bead on to the thread then slip the
needle through the leather or ribbon. Continue
threading beads and slipping the needle through
the leather or ribbon as shown in the diagram,
until you get to the end of the belt. Fasten off the
thread, and sew a press stud on to the ends to
fasten the belt.

7. Facing Facts

Our faces are the most important parts of our bodies with regard to looks. They reveal our moods and expressions, and thus look beautiful or ugly as much for those reasons as for their actual shape. So we owe it to ourselves and our friends to make the most of our faces and look after them as well as possible.

Healthy skin

For skin to look good it has to be healthy, and it will only be healthy if you are in good health too. So you need to eat the right things (you will find more about diet on page 114), to get plenty of exercise, preferably in the open air, to get as much fresh air as possible, and to get enough sleep — about eight hours a night is the average amount people need. The skin renews itself during sleep, which is why, if you have too many late nights, it doesn't look too good.

It is also important to keep your skin clean. You may use a cleansing lotion or prefer to wash your face in soap and water, but if you do the latter it is best to use a mild, unperfumed soap and wash gently with the fingertips, rinsing the soap off with plenty of clean water. If you don't like soap but still like the refreshing feel of water, make yourself some washing grains. Dry some orange peel in the oven and grind it up finely in a coffee grinder. Combine one part of the ground peel with two parts of oatmeal, and mix this with enough water to make a paste. Dab it all over your face with your fingertips, then rinse it off thoroughly. You could use oatmeal on its own, but the addition of orange peel makes the mixture smell delicious and feel more refreshing.

If you wear make-up then all traces of it must be removed each day. Eye make-up needs special remover cream or lotion, for if you try to wash it off you will be left with a horrible mess all over your face, and on the face cloth, too, if you use one.

Using a toner makes your skin feel clean and refreshed. You could use rose water, which you can buy at a chemist's, or, for greasy skin, rose water mixed with witch hazel. The latter can also be bought at a chemist, and makes an excellent eye lotion, too. An alternative toner can be made with half a cucumber, put through a liquidizer, mixed with two tablespoons of witch hazel.

Mud packs can be applied to the skin to help remove dead cells on the surface, and leave the skin glowing. Proprietary brands can be bought, but you can make your own more cheaply by buying a small quantity of kaolin or Fuller's earth from the chemist and mixing it to a paste with water. Spread it on your face and leave to dry for twenty minutes or so before washing it off. It is as well to apply a mud pack when you know no one will call, for if you have to go to the door with it on you will feel rather silly, and might frighten your visitor! Yoghurt also makes a good, cleansing face mask, and is excellent for clearing up blemishes like spots and blackheads.

Finally, if your skin tends towards dryness, or if you are out a lot in the sun, or in cold winds, your skin may need a moisturizing cream. This puts back into the skin the oils that are washed out, and which get dried out by central heating and weather. It also acts as a barrier, keeping the drying agents from absorbing the skin's natural oils and moisture. You can make your own moisturizing creams, but they tend to need rather special ingredients, so it is probably better to buy a skin cream from a chemist.

Eyes

If you are tired, and your eyes are sore from doing too much homework – or watching too much television – then cold tea or cucumber make excellent remedies. Dip pieces of cotton wool into cold tea and then rest them on your eyelids, or you can simply put used, cold teabags on your eyelids. Lie down for as long as you can, and your eyes will feel wonderfully refreshed. Or, if you prefer to use cucumber, slice it and lay the slices on your eyelids in a similar way. It feels lovely and cool, and is very soothing for tired eyes.

Mouth

I'm sure you know you should clean your teeth properly at least twice a day, but did you know that a little salt, or a little bicarbonate of soda, mixed with water, makes a good toothpaste? And if you're worried about your breath, especially if you have been eating strongly flavoured foods like garlic, chewing parsley is a very good remedy.

Hands

It's no use looking attractive, wearing your snazziest clothes and having immaculate make-up and a super hairstyle if your hands and nails let you down. Keep them clean, and try not to bite your nails. Push down the cuticles when the skin is soft after washing or bathing, to stop them splitting. Don't grow your nails too long, or they will break and look awful. File them into an attractive oval shape using an emery board, working from the sides towards the centre. Wear gloves when you are out in cold weather, especially if your skin is dry, or you may get nasty sore cracks in your hands. For the same reason you should wear rubber gloves when doing any chores that involve keeping your hands in water for any length of time, such as washing-up. If the skin on your hands feels dry and stretched, rub hand cream in as often as possible, especially after washing. Glycerine and rosewater hand lotion is good. You can buy it ready mixed, or you can make your own from one part of glycerine to two parts of rosewater.

Make-up

Make-up should be used to camouflage your worst points and bring out your best ones. If you are pale, you can use it to give you a healthy glow; if your skin is not as smooth and unblemished as you would like it to be, you can use it to hide the blemishes. But you can also use it to create an illusion of your face being a different, and more ideal, shape than it really is.

If your face is long, apply highlighter above the eyebrow and below the eye in a V shape, and put blusher over the cheekbones.

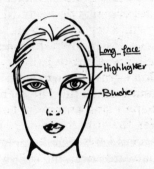

If your face is square, apply highlighter in a line high up on the cheekbones, and put a dark shader on the point of the jaw, under the cheekbones, and radiating up from the end of the eyebrow. Apply blusher over the cheekbones.

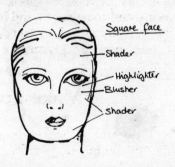

If your face is round, put highlighter radiating up from the end of the eyebrows and again in a line from just below the eye. Put shader between these two lines, radiating up and outwards from the centre of the eyebrows, and under the cheekbones. Put blusher over the cheekbones.

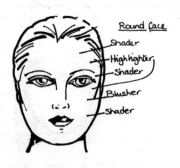

If your face is heart-shaped, apply shader radiating up and outwards from the centre of the eyebrows, and a little under the cheekbones, with just a touch of highlighter above the cheekbones. Apply blusher over the cheekbones.

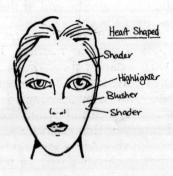

If your face is oval, which is considered the most perfect shape, then put highlighter above the eyebrow and below the eye in a V shape, and shader below the cheekbones. Apply blusher over the cheekbones.

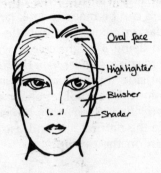

A good trick for all face types is to apply two shades of blusher that tone together, with the darker shade in the centre, so the more intense colour centres over the cheekbones and then fades to a paler colour.

Lipstick

If you wear lipstick, you will get a truer colour if you apply it over foundation. To get a pouting look, wear a darker shade of lipstick on the upper lip than on the lower. You can create all kinds of interesting effects by drawing an outline round the lips in a different colour from the main one. A lip pencil achieves this easily. You can experiment with brownish colours, or plum-toned ones, and use a more ordinary shade for the main colour. If you like your lips to shine, apply lip gloss over your lipstick. Or if you like a natural shiny effect, wear lip gloss on its own.

Large, full lips can be made to look narrower by outlining just inside the natural line with a darker shade than the main one. It is best not to use lip gloss, for this will make the lips look larger.

Thin lips can be made to look larger by outlining with a darker colour just outside the natural line, and then using a bright colour with lots of gloss.

If your top lip is thinner than the bottom one, outline it just outside the natural line, and fill in with a bright colour. Use a lighter shade on the lower lip.

If your top lip is thicker than the bottom one, outline it outside the natural line and use a darker lipstick on it than on the top lip.

Eye make-up

You can have more fun with eye make-up than with any other kind. Stunning effects can be created if you are adventurous and use two or more colours of eye shadow at the same time. Below are some ways in which you can enhance your natural looks – and create unashamedly unnatural ones, too!

Deep set eyes can be made to look less so by the use of pale eye shadow on the lids, and by using coloured rather than black mascara.

Closely set eyes can be improved by using pale shadow on the inner corners of the lids and darker shadow on the outer corners.

Widely set eyes need a strong colour on the inner corners of the lids, and may have a lighter one on the outer corners.

Small eyes look larger if softly coloured shadow is

used, with a little under the bottom lashes as well as on the eyelid. Black mascara should be avoided, and brown, grey or brownish-black mascara used instead.

Protruding eyes are helped by putting a lot of soft colour on the lid and smudging it with your finger-tips. A little can be put below the eyes too.

A soft plum-coloured shadow at the inner and outer corners, with a paler, pinkish shade in the centre, looks pretty.

Yellow shadow can be used above blue or green, with eyeliner of the opposite colour, to create an eye-catching effect.

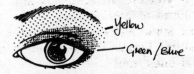

For a sophisticated, sultry effect, use a pinkish brown shadow in the inner corner of the lid, blending to grey-blue, with dark brown at the outer corners. Charcoal grey eyeliner completes the picture.

A lighter effect can be created using a soft chestnut brown lightly over the whole upper lid, with a darker brown sweeping away from the outer corner. A similar effect could be created with a pale and a darker blue, or a light and a charcoal grey.

Soft Chestnut Brown

Darker Brown

Gold or silver shadow on the inner parts of the lid, shading to reddish-brown or mauve, can look stunning. The eyeliner (brown or mauve) should be applied more thickly along the lower lashes than the upper.

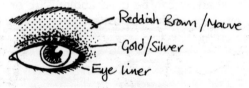

Reddish Brown /Mauve

Gold /Silver

Eye liner

For a sensational party effect, take the shadow below your eyes and fill in above right to the eyebrow, shading to a darker colour in the outer corner. You could even colour your eyebrows to match. It would look stunning in a strong blue, green, pink or lilac, to match your clothes.

Lighter Shade
Darker Shadow

Party Time

Here are some ideas for make-up for special occasions. They are not for the faint-hearted, though!

Try echoing your eyebrow arches with a row of glittering dots produced from glitter eyeshadow, or even lipstick (see illustration 1).

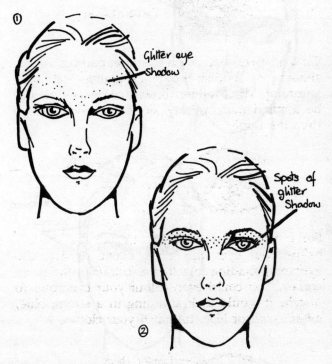

Glitter eye shadow

Spots of glitter shadow

Fill in the whole area between your eyes and the eyebrows with spots of different coloured eyeshadow, including gold, silver, red, blue and green (see illustration 2).

Make a dramatic 'mask' out of dark shadow all round the eyes (illustration 3). Sprinkle gold dust on your forehead, and use a gold-toned lipstick.

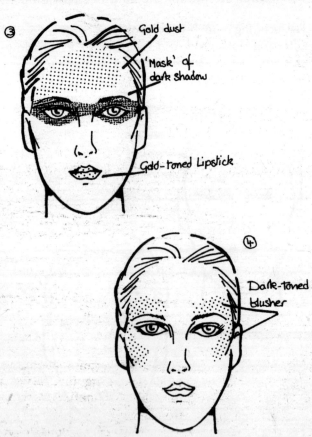

Using a darkish-toned blusher, put an arc of colour over your eyebrows, and a matching one over your cheekbones (illustration 4).

Put dark grey shadow round your eyes and shade it to silver in the underbrow area. Wear a dark plum lipstick with silver tones to match.

⑤

Silver shadow

Dark grey Shadow

Dark plum lipstick with Silver tone

Nails

Even if you don't usually wear nail varnish, you can have fun painting your nails for a special occasion. Try painting each nail a different colour (if your friends have the same idea you can share the cost of buying lots of different colours). Or, if you have lots of patience and a steady hand, paint a pattern on your nails. Here are some you might like to try.

2 tones   Spots   Strips   4 tones

8. Hair Today

Never before have people had so much choice over how to wear their hair. You can have it short, long or medium-length, a mass of curls or poker straight, elaborately styled and coloured, or just left in its natural state — and still be in fashion. The choices are so many that they can be bewildering in themselves. But whatever you choose, for it to look at its best in any style, your hair must be healthy.

Tips for Healthy Hair

Here are some of the ways to ensure that your hair will be in tip-top condition.

Diet

For your hair to look healthy you too have to be healthy, and a large part of good health depends on your diet, i.e. what you eat and drink every day. You should make sure that at every meal you eat some *protein*, which is found in meat, fish, eggs, cheese, milk, beans, nuts, and in less concentrated forms in cereals such as wheat and maize. You should also eat some fresh fruit and/or fresh salads or vegetables, which are high in

114

vitamins, and some *roughage*, such as wholemeal bread or pasta, or cereal products. This will give you a balanced diet, with all the nutrients, vitamins and minerals you need to keep healthy. To be certain that your diet is balanced, try to eat different things on different days. You should also make sure that you drink plenty of water, not just endless cups of tea or coffee or fizzy drinks.

Shampoo

Hair has to be kept clean for it to look good, and there is a huge variety of shampoos from which to choose. Finding the right one can often be a matter of trial and error. In general, though, the milder shampoos seem to give the best results, as even if you have greasy hair, those shampoos formulated specially to remove the grease often seem to leave the scalp dry and itchy. Unless your hair is very dirty it is best to apply just one lot of shampoo after wetting the hair thoroughly, and rub it well into the scalp, washing the ends more lightly, especially if you have long hair. It should then be rinsed thoroughly until it squeaks when rubbed between thumb and fingers.

If you use a conditioner this can then be applied (with greasy hair it is as well to apply it just to the ends) and combed through gently before rinsing once more. When your hair is wet it is more vulnerable to damage from combs and brushes, so treat it with care. Squeeze the water out and then wrap your hair in a towel, squeezing it gently again to take out the water. Vigorous rubbing can damage the hair. Similarly, when you comb through your wet hair, do it gently.

Hair Problems

Dryness

If your hair is very dry, use one of the rich, creamy shampoos specially made for dry hair. Try to avoid washing it too often, and brush it every day, holding your head forwards, with long strokes right from the roots. The brushing will stimulate the oil glands and should help to make the hair less dry. You could also try rubbing warmed olive oil into your scalp and wrapping your head in a towel for half an hour or so before you wash your hair. Hot sunshine, cold winter winds, perms, streaking and colouring, heated rollers, styling brushes, and hot hairdryers all tend to make the hair dry, so avoid them as much as you can. Try to wear a hat or scarf when you are out in the sun and wind, and let your hair dry naturally whenever possible. Use a conditioner specially formulated for dry hair every time you wash your hair, and if you use styling mousses and gels, make sure they are suitable for use on dry hair.

Greasiness

It is said that if you resist the temptation to wash greasy hair every other day or so, and leave it for weeks, the condition cures itself, but I suspect few people could bear to try it out! For most people the answer is to wash it as often as it needs washing, using a mild shampoo with one application only, for washing the grease out too vigorously seems to stimulate still more. A final rinse with a dessert-spoon of lemon juice (for blonde hair) or vinegar

116

(for dark hair) added to the water will help. Conditioners should only be used on the ends of the hair, and it is best to avoid brushing altogether, for it will stimulate the oil glands still more and make matters worse. The same things that make dry hair over-dry can help to make greasy hair less greasy, so you might find that, for example, having a perm helps.

Dandruff

Dandruff is small flakes of dead skin which you may see in your hair, or on your shoulders when you wear dark clothing. It is often caused by using too harsh a shampoo, or by not rinsing your hair thoroughly when you wash it, or it may simply be a reaction to poor diet, ill health or stress. There are lots of anti-dandruff shampoos on the market, so if changing to a mild shampoo doesn't help, see if the condition can be improved with one of these. For really severe conditions, you could consult a trichologist − a hair specialist − who will be able to advise you.

Split ends

Split ends usually occur in long hair when the tips of the hairs have become very dry and porous. They start with a little whitish tip which turns into a split and can travel right up the hair shaft, dividing it in two. The only cure is to have your hair trimmed, though you can buy shampoos that claim to 'mend' the hair, as a temporary solution. To avoid getting split ends in the first place, treat your hair gently. Use a brush with round-ended bristles, and a comb with widely spaced teeth, which will not pull the hair, and try to avoid combing it when it is wet. Using too many colouring products on the hair can pre-dispose it to having split ends, as can too much perming, and using too many heated rollers, brushes, and hot hairdryers.

Growing your hair

If you have had your hair cut short and layered, and then decide that what you really want is long hair all the same length, then you need to be patient. Hair grows at the rate of approximately 1cm per month (though some people's hair grows faster than others'), so it may take two years or more before you get the desired effect! To make it bearable during this time, you will probably need to have it trimmed regularly, for as a layered style grows out of its original shape it can look awful, and that won't make you feel any better about it!

If you want to cheat, you could always buy a wig or a hairpiece, though these are not cheap. The latest way to cheat is to have a hair extension. Artificial fibres coloured to match your hair are bonded to your natural hair by means of a heat-sealing device, and the 'hair' can then be washed and set like ordinary hair, though heated rollers and hot hairdryers have to be handled with care, or the fibres can melt! Your natural hair has to be at least 8cm long for the process to work, and you have to have it done in a hairdressing salon, so it isn't cheap.

Perming

Perming your hair should not be undertaken lightly, for its effects last until the hair that has been permed is cut off. But it can make a great difference to a style, and give bounce and shape to otherwise limp, lank hair. There are lots of different types of perms, depending on the effect you want and your kind of hair. The best thing to do, if you think you want a perm, is to talk it over with your hairdresser, who should advise you on the best kind of perm to have.

After perming

You shouldn't wash your hair for two days after having a perm, nor brush or comb it too vigorously, for these will all tend to drag out the curl. Hairdressers advise regular conditioning of permed hair, and using styling mousse after washing. It is best to use only gentle heat if you dry it using a hairdryer, and if possible, you should use a diffuser to stop a jet of air blowing hard in one place. Ideally you should let the hair dry naturally, tipping your head upside down every so often to give root lift to the hair. It will still need regular trimming every month or so to keep it in shape.

Colouring

Hair colorants fall into three categories: permanent, semi-permanent, and temporary. The temporary ones — those that you either spray on, or shampoo in — are best to start with, for then, if you don't like the result, you can wash it out again. Semi-permanent colours last for between three and twelve shampoos, depending on your hair and the product you choose, so if you make a mistake it isn't *too* drastic. But permanent colours are just that, and can only be got rid of by cutting off the hair or dyeing it a different colour, so they should be used with caution. The same applies to bleaching. With both of these operations there is also the problem of hair growth. After only a week you may notice that the roots are showing through with your hair's natural colour, and if you don't re-colour them you will end up with two-tone hair — OK if you want to look punk but not if you don't!

Any kind of colouring, if done repeatedly, can damage the hair, so make sure you use a good conditioner to keep your hair looking shiny and healthy.

Streaking

Colouring small sections of your hair is called highlighting if you lighten, or reduce the colour, and lowlighting if you add colour. It is a good way of adding interest to your hair colour without having to worry about constantly touching up the different coloured roots as the hair grows. Because the colour is not added all over, it tends to blend in in a natural-looking way.

Streaking is not easy to do at home, and impossible without the help of a friend, but because it is expensive to have done in a salon you could have a go if you have a willing helper. You could return the favour by doing her hair afterwards. You need to think carefully first about the colour (or colours, because you don't necessarily have to confine yourself to one) you are going to use. You will have to buy a permanent dye, or all your friend's hard work will wash out in a week or two, so it is important that you get the shade right. Streaking can be done along the whole length of the hair, from root to tip, or just at the ends if you have short hair.

There are two basic methods of streaking hair. One uses a tightly-fitting plastic cap, which you put on your head, and through which your helper pulls a number (between fifty and sixty is usual) tiny sections of hair with a crochet hook. This is not easy to do, and can be uncomfortable for the person undergoing the treatment, though you can buy streaking kits which include a cap marked with circles through which the hair is pulled, which helps. The other method uses sheets of aluminium foil, or even cling-film, though this can be awkward to handle, and small sections of the hair are wrapped in the foil like little parcels.

Cap method

Cover your head with the tightly-fitting plastic cap, making sure that all the hair is tucked underneath. Your helper then has to make small holes all over the cap about 2–3cm apart and pull through a few hairs at each hole. The hair colour or bleach is then mixed according to the manufacturer's instructions, and applied to the strands of hair with a small sponge, old toothbrush, or wad of cotton wool. The helper should wear rubber

1. *Cover head with tightly fitting plastic cap. Use a hairpin or crochet hook to make the holes and pull hairs through, keeping strands as fine as possible.*
2. *Prepare bleach colour according to manufacturers' instructions and apply liberally. Cover hair with plastic bag.* **3.** *Rinse thoroughly once bleach/colour has taken effect, leaving on plastic cap.*

gloves while doing this, and note the time. The whole head is then covered in a plastic bag, and you have to wait until the colour or bleach has taken effect. It takes about twenty minutes, but check the instructions with your particular product and time it carefully. When the time is up, the plastic bag is removed and the hair rinsed thoroughly, still keeping the plastic cap on so no colour seeps through to the rest of the hair. When all the colour or bleach has been well rinsed off, the cap is removed, and the hair shampooed as usual. You can, at this stage if you like, wash in a non-permanent colour to tone down any over-brightness, and to add interest to the rest of your hair.

Foil method

Prepare fifty to sixty pieces of foil, each a little longer than your hair and about 6cm wide. Then divide the hair all over the head into sections, pinning it up with clips or grips. Starting with the lowest hair at the back, and gradually working towards the centre of the scalp, select a few hairs at 2–3cm intervals, lay each section on a piece of foil, and apply the ready-prepared colour. Again, note the time when you start. Fold the edges of the foil in towards the centre, two to three times, from both the sides and the end, and pinch the foil at the top to stop the colour seeping out. Work all round the head in this way. When the processing time is complete, start unwrapping the foil in the place where you started, then rinse thoroughly and shampoo as before.

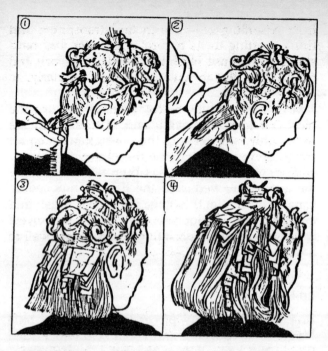

1. *Divide hair into sections.* **2.** *Starting with the lowest hairs, lay a few on foil and apply ready-prepared colour.* **3.** *Fold over sides of foil and pinch at top to stop colour seeping out. Gradually work to centre of scalp, selecting a few hairs at 2–3cm intervals.* **4.** *Work all around head in this way.*

Black hair

Black hair can often be dry and fragile, and needs careful handling. It is best to use a mild shampoo and conditioner on it, and to give it regular moisturizing treatments with a light oil. Reversion-resistant hair sprays will help to prevent the hair from absorbing moisture in the atmosphere and thus reverting to its natural state after you have styled it. Because black hair tends to be dry and brittle, it is best to have it trimmed regularly, to avoid split ends.

Black hair can also be coloured, as can oriental hair. But in both cases it is best to stick to the reddish or burgundy shades, which will impart attractive warm highlights, than to try the lighter colours, which may well result in the hair looking an unattractive brassy shade.

Because oriental hair is straight, thick and glossy, it often looks best worn long, or twisted into an elegant chignon. But it also adapts well to a straight, blunt-cut bob.

Straightening

It is better to have black hair straightened in a salon, where they will know how to take proper care of it. But you can make a temporary straightening effect using curling tongs. First divide the hair, which should be clean and dry, into sections and pin or clip them out of the way. Apply conditioner, section by section, to the whole length of the hair. Then gently but firmly smooth and straighten the hair section by section with the tongs. You can then either leave the hair gently curved, or curl it with the tongs into your pre-ferred style.

Perming

It may seem silly to perm black hair, but it can be done, if care is taken to protect it from too harsh a treatment. Perming removes some of the hair's natural curl, and makes the resulting curls softer and more manageable.

Long hair can be straightened, then swept up into this elegant style, in which the ends are curled and pinned over the front of the head and forehead. For a special occasion, the hair at the front could be sprayed with a gold or coloured spray.

Long hair can also be pulled back into a tight pony tail, and divided into twists or plaits which are then twisted round and pinned into place. They, too, can be braided for a special effect.

Long hair that has been permed can be left to dry into natural ringlets, which can then be controlled by tying back the front and top sections with ribbon. Or the hair at the side can be combed up and pinned on top of the head.

This exciting short hairstyle is created by having a really good cut, which accentuates high cheekbones, and then straightening and styling the hair.

Styling Your Hair

If you don't have permed hair, you may want to style it after washing. This can be done in a number of ways.

Blow drying

This is used to give the hair bounce and lift, and to curve it into shape. First you need to divide the hair into sections, pinning them out of the way with hairgrips or clips while you concentrate on one part at a time. The hair at the top of your head should be pinned out of the way first, while you dry the hair that is underneath. Pick up a section of hair, wind it round the bristles of a large brush for bouncy curves, or a small brush for curls, and run the dryer over it until it is dry. Repeat the drying for each section. When you have finished, lightly brush or comb it into place.

Finger drying

This simply means running your fingers through the hair as you use a hairdryer on it, to give it root lift, and to curve the ends in the direction you want them to go.

Setting

Hair can be set by winding it on to rollers, rolling it round to make pin curls which are secured by grips, or winding it round bendy clips. It can then be dried with a hairdryer, or left to dry naturally.

Curling tongs, hot brushes and heated rollers

These can all be used to style dry hair and are useful for reviving a drooping hairstyle before you go out. As with all heat treatments, if you use these devices too often they will dry your hair, and possibly cause split ends. You can now buy hot bendy clips to style your hair, as well as tongs, brushes and rollers.

Keeping the style in place

Setting lotions, styling gels, mousses, and hair sprays will all help to keep your hair looking the way you want it. If you are worried about the use of CFCs (chlorofluorocarbons) in aerosols (and you should be, for they are damaging your world!), there are a number of products on the market now which do not use them and which are quite safe, among them being Clynol, and Sainsbury's and Safeway's own-brand hair sprays. For a complete list of safe products, write to Friends of the Earth, 26–28 Underwood Street, London N1 7JQ.

Creating a New Style

On the next few pages are some new and exciting styles for you to try. But if none of them is quite you, or if you already know what you want, go along to a recommended hairdresser and tell him or her about it. It helps to take along a photograph of the style so the hairdresser can see what you mean. Be guided by his or her advice – hairdressers often know best when it comes to deciding which styles suit a particular face or hair type.

For those who long for a new style but are unsure if it will suit them, a new service may soon be available. It consists of a computer-operated machine, which will show you as you are, and then as you might look with a whole range of changes — for example, with short blonde hair, long red hair, or medium length curly brown hair. It is available at the time of writing in the USA, but believed to be being introduced in Britain soon, so look out for it!

Here are some exciting styles you might like to try. They are divided into three sections — for short, medium-length and long hair.

Short hair

A simple, short urchin cut can be given volume and lift with styling mousse.

This sophisticated style is created by using styling mousse, blow-drying and then spraying lightly with hair spray. Earrings make the style look dressy.

If short hair is long enough on top, this terrific style can be created with heated bendy clips and firm-hold hair spray.

If you want a style that needs no attention, apart from washing, gelling and running your fingers through it, what about this unisex cut?

Medium-length hair

A simple, shoulder-length bob can be worn like this.

Or the hair can be swept over the face, like this.

Layered, medium-length hair can be set in this pretty style with rollers or bendy clips, and the fringe's kiss curls created with pin curls.

A perm, or all-over setting with rollers, will create this glamorous style.

This is a super style for thick, coarse hair cut short on top.

Long hair

If your hair is long, and all the same length, you can wear it straight and loose.

Or you can plait it in a French plait. This is done by gathering a handful of hair at the crown, dividing it into three strands, winding left over centre, then right over centre, then taking in a little more hair from each side as shown in the diagrams on pages 136 and 137. This is repeated all the way down until all the hair is gathered into the plait.

If you want to look sophisticated you can wear long hair in a French pleat. Follow the step-by-step instructions on pages 138 and 139 – it's much easier than it looks.

French plait

1 *Starting above each ear, draw your two thumbs upwards towards the centre back of your head, gathering a central section of the hair up into a pony tail.*

2 *Divide this pony tail into three.*

3 *Now start plaiting: draw the left strand over the central strand as shown.*

4 *Cross the right strand over the new central strand.*

5 *Hold the plait in your right hand, using your fingers to keep the three strands separate.*

6 *Now use your left thumb to draw a new strand of hair – a little thinner than the original strands – towards your unfinished plait.*

7 *Add the new strand to the original left strand. Cross this thicker strand into the centre, and take the centre strand in your left hand as shown.*

8 *Next, hold the plait in your* left *hand, using your fingers to keep the three strands separate.*

9 *Use your* right *thumb this time to draw the new, thinner, strand of hair towards the main plait.*

10 *Add the new strand to the original* right *strand, and cross this thicker strand to the centre. Take the centre strand into your right hand as shown.*

11 *Continue taking hair from the left and right (steps 5–10) until there is no loose hair left.*

12 *Plait the remaining length in the normal way. This is the finished look.*

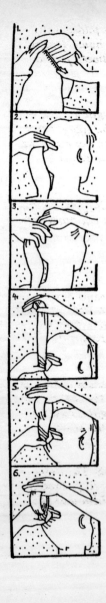

French pleat

1 *With your left hand, gather the hair into . . .*

2 *a pony tail.*

3 *Twist the pony tail all the way round once, so that its base is tight against your head.*

4 *Holding the base of the pony tail tightly with your left hand, twist the end upwards as shown.*

5 *Fold the end of the pony tail downwards, about one third of the way.*

6 *Fold the whole pony tail down again, catching the bottom end in your right hand.*

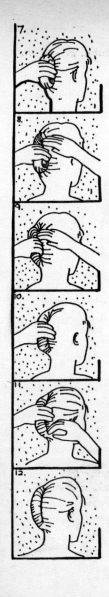

7 *Catch the whole folded pony tail in your left hand, leaving a little space between it and your head.*

8 *Now you can begin to tuck the pony tail into the space. Start at the top and gently push the hair in with your fingers, as shown.*

9 *Work downwards, pushing the hair under your left hand into the space.*

10 *Nearly there! You have now pushed the whole pony tail into the space, and your hair is forming a tight roll.*

11 *Now secure the seam with hair pins starting at the bottom. Push them in tight along the whole length of the seam.*

12 *The finished look! The hair-pins should be well pushed in to keep them hidden and the pleat tight.*

For a special evening, how about this medieval look. You need a friend to help you create it, but it is very pretty.

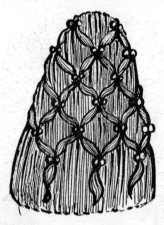

Or you can have long hair permed, to give this fantastic effect. For waves rather than curls, you could simply plait it when wet.

If you really want to create a stir and your hair is short on top, gel it into spikes for this fantastic look.

You can have a lot of fun experimenting with different hair styles, different make-up, different clothes and different 'looks'. Don't be afraid to experiment, and don't be afraid of making mistakes, for it is only by trying out new things that you will discover what really suits you and what you look really good in. Your clothes should feel as if they are part of your personality, and you should feel comfortable in them, for no one ever looks right if they don't feel right.

From your experiments you may discover that you like and look good in a particular style of clothes, or in certain colours, or you may feel that you want to keep changing your image. And why not, if that is what you want to do? Nowadays, more than ever before, people have the freedom to wear what they please. You can follow other people's styles or create your own, look formal, decorative, or functional – or all three, on different days of the week. Don't take it too seriously, for above all, you should enjoy your clothes, and have fun with your experiments and ideas. That is what fashion is all about.

ACTIVITY BOOKS

If you enjoy making and doing fun things, perhaps you ought to try some of our exciting activity books. They are available in bookshops or they can be ordered directly from us. Just complete the form below and enclose the right amount of money and the books will be sent to you at home.

☐ THINGS TO MAKE IN THE HOLIDAYS	Steve and Megumi Biddle	£1.99
☐ CRAZY COOKING	Juliet Bawden	£2.25
☐ CRAZY PUPPETS	Delphine Evans	£1.95
☐ THINGS TO MAKE FOR CHRISTMAS	Eric Kenneway	£1.95
☐ THE PAPER JUNGLE	Satoshi Kitamura	£2.75
☐ SPRING CLEAN YOUR PLANET	Ralph Levinson	£1.75
☐ HOW TO MAKE SQUARE EGGS	Paul Temple and Ralph Levinson	£1.50
☐ COACHING TIPS FROM THE STARS: SOCCER	David Scott	£1.99
☐ FREAKY FASHIONS	Caroline Archer	£1.95

If you would like to order books, please send this form, and the money due to:
ARROW BOOKS, BOOKSERVICE BY POST, PO BOX 29, DOUGLAS, ISLE OF MAN, BRITISH ISLES. Please enclose a cheque or postal order made out to Arrow Books Ltd for the amount due including 22p per book for postage and packing both for orders within the UK and for overseas orders.

NAME ....

ADDRESS ....

....

Please print clearly.

Whilst every effort is made to keep prices low it is sometimes necessary to increase cover prices at short notice. Arrow Books reserve the right to show new retail prices on covers which may differ from those previously advertised in the text or elsewhere.